Activate Your Life Vol. III

23 transformational exercises from
coaches all over the world

First Printing 2021

ISBN: 9798750767731

Published by

The Art of Adventure

146 Helfenstein Ave

St. Louis, MO 63119

Derekloudermilk.com

The ART Of

Edited by Word and Wing

wordandwing.co

WORD & WING

Disclaimer:

This book is not intended as a substitute for the medical advice of physicians. The reader should regularly consult a physician in matters relating to his/her health and particularly with respect to any symptoms that may require diagnosis or medical attention. The information provided in Activate You Life is for educational and informational purposes only, and is made available to you as self-help tools for your own use. The Authors cannot and do not guarantee that you will attain a particular result, and you accept and understand that results differ by each individual.

TABLE OF CONTENTS

By Paul Cantrell

INTRODUCTION

This is the third volume in the *Activate Your Life* series, and this is a book with a mission. That mission is to bring the best exercises for the healing, evolution, and unity of humanity. After two years of upheaval, the pandemic, civil unrest, and societal collapse, we knew that we needed to step up our game with this book - to help the world heal, and more importantly, to help create the world how *we* really want it to be, from a place of peace, alignment, and consciousness.

Activate Your Life was born as a project to share the work of amazing coaches. I was living in Bali at the time and many of the initial authors were my mentors, coaches, and healers. I would bring them in to teach sessions at my AdventureQuest retreats and the experiences they created would blow people away. I wanted a way to bring those experiences to the world, and also help my friends become published authors.

At the time, I was part of a collaborative book project where 100 entrepreneurs shared a key business lesson in their own chapter in *The Better Business Book*. The book became a bestseller and gave me the confidence to publish my first solo book, *Superconductors*. I realized how a collaborative book project like this could grow community, demystify the publishing world, and build confidence in the authors.

As the host of *The Derek Loudermilk Show* podcast, I see it as my job to bring cutting-edge ideas and thought leaders to my audience, and the *Activate Your Life* book series is a beautiful complement. In *Activate Your Life Volume III*, you will encounter the leading minds in the coaching, healing, and metaphysical worlds.

When I first started as an entrepreneur more than a decade ago, a few simple exercises changed my life. One such exercise was to envision my perfect day in detail. Three years later, I was watching the sunset over the Adriatic Sea with my family, and I realized that I had just lived out that exact perfect day. Going through just one exercise can truly *activate your life.*

How to use this book

We have broken down the content into different sections with certain themes – I recommend going straight to the section that most interests you or where you think you can find the biggest benefit.

You can learn something or you can *know* something. To truly know something, you must have a lived experience - so, these exercises are all about action. You "work through" them. You will get the biggest benefit by setting aside some time and completing an exercise. If you don't set aside time to do them, you will simply be getting more information and ideas.

It can help to know that when you are working on a transformational process, it will likely feel uncomfortable. This is because your brain is working hard to create new connections as you learn, your worldview may be shifting, and you may have to use courage if you face challenging truths. Anytime our physical body or thoughts are changed, it interrupts the careful balance called homeostasis, which takes energy. Learn to embrace this discomfort or struggle, because this means the exercises are working!

To keep your momentum, it can help to have a strong emotional attachment with the outcome you are seeking. Check back in with *why* you are doing these exercises in the first place. What is the vision you see for yourself? Who needs you to show up and do your best with these exercises?

If you are a coach, welcome! After starting this project, the authors soon discovered that we were excited to learn and use everyone else's exercises. Please feel free to try out, use, and adapt these exercises with your own clients. I've heard from hundreds of coaches that use the *Activate Your Life* books as a reference guide to find the right exercise for any coaching situation. You can even build out the curriculum for your events and retreats using these exercises. If you would like to republish any particular exercise, please contact the individual author.

This book gives you access to a team of the world's top coaches, in the comfort of your own home. This is a great book to bring to your mastermind or networking group or do with an accountability buddy. As with the African proverb, "To go fast, go alone. To go far, go with friends".

You can go far with this book, but if you are truly motivated to transform your life, I encourage you to seek continued support from coaches. All of our authors offer additional training and programs, so if you want more from a particular coach, please visit their website or email them directly.

We hope *Activate Your Life Volume III* will help you break through your most pressing challenges and guide you to achieve your biggest goals.

The world needs you, now more than ever

Derek Loudermilk

October 7, 2021

PART 1
SUPER YOU:

MASTERING YOUR THOUGHTS AND EMOTIONS

What Would Super-You Do? Use Archetypes to Make Decisions From Your Best Self

By Cassa Grant

Anyone who gets stuck in 'the weeds' and has a hard time making decisions from their best self will benefit from this exercise. By encouraging you to step outside of yourself and into an archetype, you'll boost your confidence, create a higher vision to work towards, and start being the person you want to be in a tangible, actionable way.

Great for:

- Those who struggle with decision-making and procrastinate over life choices, big or small.

- Wanting to feel more confident and empowered when approaching challenges.

- Strategies to stop you from sabotaging your own goals and dreams.

When I worked with my first transformational coach, he'd say, "You have to *be* the person who already has the thing you want." Intellectually, I kind of understood this. But practically it made no sense to me. How could I *be* someone when I didn't have the experience to understand how they'd think, feel, or act?

The answer is to use archetypes. Archetypes are images, figures, character types, settings, and story patterns that are universally shared by people across cultures and that play a role in influencing human behavior. They were introduced by the Swiss psychiatrist Carl Jung. We're born with these archetypes, and they're reinforced through our interactions with other people as we grow and learn. Jung suggested that these archetypes were forms of innate human understanding passed down from our ancestors.

Some examples of archetypes are:

- Warrior

- Caregiver

- Everyman (guy/girl next door)

- Rebel

- Lover

- Hero

- Magician

- Sage

- Jester

- Ruler

- Explorer

When you read this list, you probably have images or people pop into your head. Archetypes are immediately understood at a deep level because they tap into how we make meaning based on a shared understanding.

Later, when I began coaching my own clients, I used Jung's theory of archetypes to help them step outside themselves and embody the person they wanted to *be* on a very fundamental, tangible level. Todd Hermann's excellent book, *The Alter Ego Effect,* details a comprehensive method of using archetypes to guide clients to meaningful change. The way I use it is simpler and is designed to work in 1-1 coaching sessions.

Because archetypes are deeply understood, we can immediately step into a way of *being* which embodies the qualities of that archetype. It's easier to think of the traits from the perspective of a personal hero, superhero, or celebrity as your subconscious mind doesn't throw up as much resistance.

Your current identity isn't bad; it might just be limited, and embodying an archetype can help you expand those limits. It inspires the imagination and keeps you motivated. Whatever you think you're lacking, you can gain through stepping into an archetype.

Being 'Super-You' isn't the same as faking it

I *hate* the phrase, "fake it 'til you make it." The whole idea behind this saying is that if you get out there and do the work, you'll start to feel more confident and grow out of your fears and lack of confidence. And that's fine – getting into action *will* make you more confident, and you do need to have the courage to start.

But manufacturing (or faking) confidence and expertise won't deal with the root cause of your problem. It will just keep you feeling like a fraud – an imposter – constantly unsure of your performance.

What can be more helpful? Embodying an alter-ego (or Super-You) based on a universal archetype. By identifying yours, you will:

- Understand how to act based on what you think your alter-ego would do.

- Start to become that alter-ego.

- Boost your confidence, *not* your Imposter Syndrome.

My alter egos have been:

- Judge Judy (when I was a young, new teacher and needed to feel authoritative and wise).

- Wonder Woman (when I was an adventure travel bus driver and had to solve any and every problem).

- My grandma (when I sometimes struggle to be as generous and grounded as I want to be).

And they've each helped me grow exponentially.

I'm not advocating for lying or being pompous – that's what I hate about the "fake it 'til you make it" mantra. But I *am* suggesting you trick your brain by pretending to *be* your alter-ego. It will allow you to embody more confidence, which helps you:

- Gain credibility.

- Make strong first impressions.

- Deal with pressure.

- Tackle personal and professional challenges.

- Make decisions based on your higher self, not your tunnel-vision, freaked-out self.

It's also an attractive trait because it helps put others at ease. Artists have been using alter-egos to boost confidence and access a higher side of themselves for decades. Think David Bowie as Ziggy Stardust, Prince as Camille, and The Beatles as Sgt. Pepper's Lonely Hearts Club Band.

One of my favorite examples is Beyoncé's 'Sasha Fierce'. When I first heard that she uses Sasha Fierce to become the performer she wants to be on stage, I was like, "Uh, seriously, Bey?" It seemed a bit over the top.

But as I've learned more about positive psychology and transformational coaching, I understand just how helpful embodying an alter-ego can be. It's a practical way (which is what I'm all about!) for people to step into being the highest version of themselves. And that's nothing to be sneezed at. Because our highest self is hiding in what we perceive as our current identity.

For example, I've had people say things to me like: "Other people are naturally good at leading [or fill in the blank], but that's not me. I didn't have brothers or sisters. I didn't grow up as 'the bossy one'. I really don't know what I'm doing. Everyone can see it."

Well, maybe they can see it, and maybe they can't. But as long as you keep *telling* yourself a story about why you aren't as good a leader as people who are bossy or people who grew up with brothers and sisters, guess what? You won't be.

So I want you to tell yourself a different story. That way you'll change yourself on a subconscious *and* conscious level. And you'll start seeing yourself as the person who can solve your own problems.

How do you rewrite the story? You discover your super-you.

Having an alter-ego you feel truly represents who you are and what you're capable of will help you step into your power and be the best version of yourself every day.

The Exercise: Part 1

Note: I've structured this for a coach having a session with a client, and listed the questions that you would ask to capture the essence of the 'Super-You'. However, this can be done individually as a journaling exercise.

1. Set the stage and the desired state of *being*

Imagine 3 years have passed and we bump into each other on the street. You say to me, "Wow, Cassa! The last 3 years have been amazing! Let me tell you about them."

What would have happened? How would you have become a better person, or leader, or parent? What would be happening in your life?

How will you know when you've got what you want? What will you see, hear, and experience? How do you *feel*? (Go for details here)

What are 5 specific things you're grateful for these days? What would you want if you knew you couldn't fail? And what else?

What's the legacy you want to leave? (This is a big question so really dig into it and go deep for the best answers). And why do you want that?

2. Introduce archetypes

Ok, let's shift gears here. You can use an archetype to help you gain the traits that you feel when we describe the person I'll be talking to in three years. Mine's called Kickass Cass. You can base them on an archetype, a superhero, a person you find inspiring, an animal, or a powerful machine.

3. Name and define the 'Super-You'

Ok, let's name this Super-You. What should we call them? (This might need a bit of refinement. The most important thing is that it helps the client drop into the *feelings* we've articulated earlier in the session).

What does your Super-You think? Believe? Do or not do? We'll use this Super-You to help you make decisions based on who you will *be* when you have the things you described to me in the first part. They'll *be* the person who can help you make decisions based on your vision, *not* on your limitations or circumstances.

4. Define the challenge

Ok, now we're going to use your Super-You to work through a challenge you're facing. Choose a challenge that's been top-of-mind lately. Then, list all the aspects of that challenge that are relevant.

So if I chose, "My Leadership", I might list:

- Employee education

- Things are taking longer than they should

- People not talking to each other

- Everyone doing what they should be doing

Score each aspect from 0-5, with zero being the worst. We'll work with the worst one first. You might also find that the worst one will actually have a domino effect and help solve other related issues if it's solved.

What's an example of a recent event that shows this problem in action?

5. Solve the challenge as the 'Super-You'

1. Now, I want you to step into your Super-You. If Super-You had a year to come up with a plan to fix this problem, what is one thing you could come up with?

2. If Super-You had only one week to figure out a solution, what could you do to take your first idea and compress it from a year to a week?

3. Based on the first two questions, what can you go ahead and do *tomorrow* morning that would help you fix this problem? Is this a long-term solution? How can you turn it into one?

6. Integrate

What was your biggest insight from this exercise?

(Keep digging into that feeling and help your client create a strategy to tap into their 'Super-You' in other circumstances. Also, some key journaling questions will come up during the session, so we'll customarily identify those as action items to follow up on along with the plan they created.)

Case study: Sparkly Jo

My client, Jo, is a copywriter and brand consultant who went through my Wonderbrand™ program. We set up her 'Super-You' as Sparkly Jo at the beginning of our time together and she still uses it today. She says that having Sparkly Jo as a touchpoint helps her remember who she is and how she wants to be, especially when times are tough or she's experiencing her boundaries being tested.

"For me, Sparkly Jo is a higher vibrating part of me. She's always within me burning bright, but sometimes - when life triggers me or I feel knocked off-center - I disconnect from her. I know when I'm not connected to Sparkly Jo because I feel ungrounded and not confident in my professional or personal life.

But, by identifying exactly who Sparkly Jo is and how she carries herself, I've found a super easy way to *not* fall down the rabbit hole of negative self-talk or limiting beliefs. Instead, when I notice I'm ungrounded, I step into Sparkly Jo (or rather 'up to', as it feels like an energetic elevation - and it is).

As Sparkly Jo, I see things from a higher perspective. It's like I've taken myself away from the heat of the volcano's edge and I'm looking down on the bubbling lava from a neighboring mountain top. I'm calm, centered, grounded... I feel my best, most badass self. Fully accepting and okay with every facet of me. Fully empowered to tackle anything.

Once I'm embodying that fizzy, high-vibrational energy, I re-approach things. I solve problems quicker. I communicate more compassionately. And I make choices that are right for everyone involved.

In short, Sparkly Jo has helped me up-level how I show up for my clients, and how I show up for myself and loved ones."

The Journey to Empowerment: Find Inner Peace in Difficult Times
By Rong Zhao

This exercise will help you find harmony and peace to handle life's challenges. You will learn how to connect with your inner strength and power to gracefully deal with life's difficult moments.

Great for:

- Those going through any emotional struggles (e.g. depression, anxiety, sadness, anger, etc.).

- Gaining more peace and grace in challenging times.

- Feeling more empowered every day in life.

Sometimes, no matter how good we appear to others on the outside, we are consistently fighting an invisible battle within. We get overwhelmed by our negative thoughts, stressed by our fears, and trapped by our own challenging emotions. As a result, we either turn to external distractions (e.g. food, alcohol, TV, etc.) or completely shut off our feelings to seek temporary relief.

I was born and grew up in a traditional Chinese family in China. My dad is a very hard-working, but emotionally aloof Chinese father. And my mom constantly worries about everything that could go wrong in her life. Because of that, growing up I always felt very distant from them, both physically and emotionally. In my memory, I couldn't remember a time when they said "I love you" or hugged me. After their divorce, when I was at a young age, I began to feel extremely unsafe about everything in my life. Over time I developed social anxiety and low self-esteem. In school, I was always the kid hiding in the corner or quiet in a group.

In high school, I suffered from severe depression and almost committed suicide because I couldn't figure out what was wrong with me. After I moved to the United States, at 22 years old, I was still struggling with my anxiety and depression. In fact, I became even more lonely and isolated due to my very limited English proficiency and poor communication skills.

There are two reasons people change. One is *inspiration* and another is *desperation*.

At my darkest moment, when I was about to give up fighting this battle, I accidentally watched a motivational speech from TED Talks. I don't remember exactly the content, but I still remember clearly that one moment when I told myself, "Wow, I wish I could do what he's doing on the stage." With this little ray of hope and my desperation for a change – any change – I decided to give public speaking a try. Reflecting back, it was absolutely one of the scariest things I had ever done. But to me, it was my only way out.

So I decided to give it my all. Soon my commitment started to pay off. After taking public speaking classes every week for a few months, I noticed a significant increase in my confidence and self-esteem. Gradually, public speaking became my passion as I continued to improve myself and began to share my own stories to inspire others. Along the way, I discovered NLP (neuro-linguistic programming), hypnosis, energy healing, and spiritual practices. With these modalities, I began to heal myself and feel empowered in a way I had never felt before. With the desire to help others, I started to coach people and became obsessed with discovering the most powerful ways to transform people's lives.

One of the modalities I stumbled upon was a simple framework taught by a spiritual teacher, which showed me that we already have all the resources within ourselves to solve any of our problems. I fell in love with this simple and elegant framework because it's easy to practice by yourself and also improves your overall long-term well-being when done regularly. So I began to incorporate this framework into my own change processes I use with my clients, and teach it at my classes and workshops.

The reason we get stuck with our emotions is simply that we are trying to solve the wrong problem. Often when we get triggered or feel stressed, we tend to analyze the situation in our mind to find a solution or imagine the worst thing that might happen to us. However, this never works, because we can't solve an emotional problem in a logical way.

For most people, we are over-relying on our head or logical mind to solve all the problems we have. As we grew up, we learned that it's the only way to get into a good school, have a good resume, get a good job, and live a good life.

Yes, our mind is very powerful. It can solve many problems for us. That's how we evolved as a human race, learning to build tools, technologies, and machines. However, if we rely too much on the mind, it creates an imbalance within us, like a car that only has one wheel. We can't go very far with one wheel, can we?

So sometimes we need to get out of our head and connect to other parts of us to deal with our emotional struggles.

How this exercise works

There are four different parts of us that we can connect with to find the resources within us to solve our own problems:

- Mind

- Body

- Heart

- Spirit

The *mind* gives us clarity. It provides logic and intelligence. It helps us analyze and evaluate things. Our human race could not be where we are without the *mind*.

The *body* gives us connection and certainty with ourselves. It helps us be more centered and grounded. It allows us to achieve things in life and connect to the earth.

The *heart* connects us together. It brings joy, compassion, happiness, love, and gratitude. It allows us to be open and vulnerable when connecting with others around us.

The *spirit* gives us intuition. It brings a sense of freedom, creativity, and fun. If you believe in a higher power, that's your *spirit*. If you don't believe in a higher power, it can be your intuition or infinite intelligence.

The goal of this exercise is to allow you to access and integrate mind, body, heart, and spirit to create balance and harmony and find solutions to any problems you may be facing.

Steps

1. Think about something you are struggling with emotionally

Pick a moment or time when you were struggling. What emotion were you feeling? It could be fear, anxiety, anger, resentment, sadness, depression, etc. Be specific about that moment. Allow yourself to experience that moment as if it's happening now.

2. Connect with your body

Get a sense of this unwanted emotion. Notice where you are feeling it in your body. Ask yourself: what's the shape and color of this sensation?

Then breathe into the feeling 10 times, embracing the feeling. Take another 5 deep breaths. This time imagine that you're breathing in and out through the soles of your feet.

3. Connect with your heart.

Put your hand onto your heart. Notice your heart beating, and feel the warmth and love from your heart.

Use the warm feeling to guide you to a time in your life when you felt loved. It could be a time when you were with your family, friends, pets or someone who helped you in the past.

When you find that time, allow yourself to flow into it. Relive the experience in first-person and notice what it makes you feel.

4. Connect with your spirit

If you believe in a higher power (e.g., God, Universe, Source, etc.), get a sense of your connection with your higher power.

If you don't believe it, get a sense of your intuition (or sometimes we call it a 6th sense or gut feeling) or this infinite intelligence you are connected to.

Listen and receive any helpful message coming from your spirit and take in that message.

5. Connect with your mind

Watch that moment when you were struggling or triggered again. But this time, watch the movie in third-person. Notice what new insights you get by observing it from a distance.

6. Integrate

Take a nice deep breath. Allow all the tensions in your body to let go and dissolve into relaxation and peace.

Now that you have completed the exercise, it's time to use it regularly for your healing and well-being. Go to www. therongway.com for the guided meditation so you can listen to it anytime anywhere.

Case study

One time I was teaching a class on how to use this framework. During the demonstration, a woman named Linda volunteered. She was feeling a deep sense of sadness and depression. After getting to know her, I learned that she had lost a long-term relationship and her business partner at the same time. There was a lot of pain and hopelessness in her voice.

I first asked her to notice where she felt in her body when she was thinking about what happened. She felt a black heavy sensation around her chest, which surprised her. She realized that she's not her feelings because she was able to observe them.

Then I asked her to breathe into the feeling and keep breathing until she felt more centered. I could tell she was already feeling calmer. Then I guided her to connect with her heart by asking her to relive a few past moments in her life when she felt deeply loved. Her skin soon began to glow and there was a smile on her face.

Next, I asked her to connect with her higher power because I learned she's spiritual. After she connected with her higher power, she received a message from it, "You are enough". Tears came out of her eyes along with joy and a sense of relief.

Lastly, I asked her to look at the problem like watching a movie. She realized that her problem was not a problem anymore, but an opportunity. After the exercise, with a bright smile on her face, she told me, "I am feeling hopeful now." Sometimes, we have underestimated how strong we are when we tap into our power.

Tips for coaches

Some clients are either stuck in their heads or shutting off their emotions entirely. When this happens, they need to get into their body first before their heart because getting into their body is one of the fastest ways to get out of their head.

The Emotional Mastery Challenge for Infinite Success
By Sonia Singh

This exercise will help you develop the skills you need to master your emotions so you can create infinite success in your business, career, or personal life. You will learn how to name your emotions, make sense of them, and move through them with ease.

Great for:

- Transforming stressful situations into ones that move you forward.

- Developing and nurturing powerful relationships.

- Learning how to effectively respond to negative emotions so you can remove obstacles to your success.

Years ago, I was teaching a course when I encountered a colleague who liked to challenge me after every training session. He would research the topic I had just taught, copy and paste information he found on Wikipedia, and email it to me along with his questions. I would then spend a lot of time responding to his emails, citing my sources, and explaining why I teach the way I do. As he continued this behavior, my frustration towards him grew until one day I reached my breaking point and responded to him negatively. Unfortunately, this only exacerbated the situation.

The problem was I acted defensively because I was reacting to my emotions and not the situation itself. Had I paused and reflected on what was really happening, the outcome may have been different. I would have responded more graceful-ly. Emotional triggers rarely, if ever, occur due to the actual event. Most likely the event is triggering an insecurity we already feel or something that has happened in the past.

Over the next few months, I worked on observing and track-ing my emotions. I noticed certain themes and patterns emerging. When someone questioned my skills, I felt angry and threatened. I recognized that if I wanted to let go of these negative emotions, I had to start asking genuine questions out of curiosity. Was the feedback true, useful, or coming from a genuine desire to help? If the answers were no, I needed to reflect on why I was being triggered. What's actu-ally bothering me? What would happen if I wasn't bothered? If someone insisted I had pink hair (when I don't), I probably would laugh it off and continue on with my day.

By following the seven steps I share here in this chapter, I finally discovered how to manage my triggers, process my emotions, and respond effectively to any situation, even a stressful one.

When you avoid certain emotions, unresolved issues stay dormant and can silently build up over time. This can cre-ate situations where your emotions eventually run wild, as happened to me years ago with my colleague. As a result, you find yourself impulsively reacting to something some-one said or did. When you become defensive, you give up your power because the emotion drives your behavior. Be aware when this happens by becoming an observer of your own emotions. Notice when you're triggered and be silent with it. What words or actions triggered you and why? Take time for introspection before you respond. The worst thing you can do when you're emotional is to react. When we op-erate in the primal part of the brain where the fight or flight mechanism kicks in, we're no longer thinking logically. As a result, our ability to make good decisions is at risk.

The Emotional Fitness (EF) Staircase is a visual tool to help you become aware of your current feelings and access the emotions you want to experience more of.

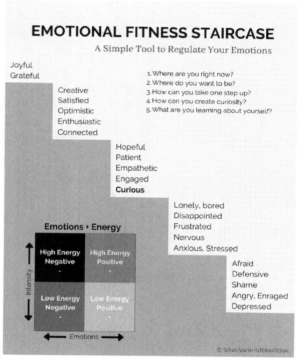

Image: Emotional Fitness Staircase

Download a copy of the Emotional Fitness Staircase at: InfluentialLeadershipAcademy.com.

The truth is that no emotion is good or bad; they're all meant to be experienced. They serve as messengers alerting us to what we need. Although they're meant to pass, sometimes we get stuck in a specific emotion, which can create suffering. When you find yourself on one of the bottom steps of the EF Staircase, it can seem daunting and unrealistic to jump to a positive mood. Instead, try getting curious. Think of curiosity as the baseline to strive for. When you're genuinely curious about a situation or the emotion, you'll start asking questions that can serve you.

As you move up the EF Staircase, the better you will feel and the higher quality thoughts you'll have. When people are in a state of joy, gratitude, and creativity, they generate the best ideas and make better decisions. It can be challenging to move from floor to floor, and it takes practice to notice which floor we've gotten off on and which one we want to head towards next. But the more you reference this staircase and name your emotions, the easier it will become for you to shift to another mood.

7 Steps to Emotional Mastery

1. Self-reflection: check in with yourself

Check in with yourself every single day. Use the EF Staircase tool as a reference to identify which emotion you're experiencing and ask yourself a few questions. Which floor am I on right now? Which floor do I visit most often? How long do I tend to stay there? Write down your thoughts on paper. Over time, you'll notice patterns emerge such as certain emotions that might be over-used, under-used, or avoided altogether.

2. Disconnect to connect: ground yourself in nature

Many scientific studies have shown that time in nature reduces stress and calms our nervous system. Even just a few minutes in nature can lower blood pressure, reduce stress hormones, increase self-esteem, and improve our mood.

Here are a few ideas to consider. Sit in the sun or take a stroll outdoors. Let your bare feet touch the grass. Open a window and feel the breeze. Look up at the infinite sky, stars, or moon and realize how massive the universe is. We are just specks on the map. The universe is so much more than us and our worries. Allow this truth to re-ground you and bring you back in touch with your heart and soul.

3. Tap into your senses: sight, hearing, touch, smell, taste

Along with spending time in nature, studies have found a healing component in the ability to use your five senses – sight, touch, sound, smell, and taste. It allows you to block out noise and refocus. Ask yourself the following questions any time you need to recenter yourself.

- What do I see around me?

- What can I touch?

- What sensations do I feel on my skin and in my body?

- What do I hear?

- What do I smell?

- What can I taste?

Here are a few ideas to consider. Breathe in fresh air. Stretch your arms, legs, neck and notice how they feel. Splash water on your face. Light a candle. Smell some flowers. Watch the clouds float by. Cuddle up in a cozy blanket.

4. Create curiosity: ask questions

If you find yourself on one of the lower floors, ask yourself questions with genuine curiosity. When we show up interested in understanding the situation, judgment seems to disappear, which is especially true when you're judging yourself. Pause and pivot to a place of curiosity.

- I wonder what this is all about?

- I wonder what this person's story is?

- I wonder what's really bothering me?

- I wonder what it is that I really want?

- What am I learning here?

- If I wasn't feeling [negative emotion], what would that look like?

- If I'm really honest with myself, what excuses am I making?

- How could this situation actually help me?

- What could I appreciate about this situation or person?

- If I were graceful, how would I respond?

Curiosity generates empathy, unlocks creativity, and moves us forward. When we begin asking questions, it's difficult to be judgemental. We become students who are on a mission to learn and expand.

5. Channel your emotions: focus on a goal

The point of our emotions isn't to have knee-jerk reactions, but to alert us. Once you understand what your emotions are trying to convey, you can decide what needs to change,

36

if anything. Lean into that pain. Use it to motivate and inspire you. Once you've created insights for yourself, you can channel that emotion. Whether it's grief, anger, or frustration, allow it to fuel you towards your goals. What do you really want? Name your goal and use it as an anchor. The majority, if not all, of the most successful and impactful people in the world were driven by powerful emotions. By learning to harness your pain for positive change, you can exponentially multiply your success.

6. Practice gratitude: create a mental shift

It's easy to get distracted by negative news, self-comparison, and other noise. But when you can shift your perspective and look at life through the lens of appreciation, your entire world changes. Make it a daily habit to think of at least one thing, event, or person you're grateful for. It becomes most powerful when you start finding the smallest reason to be grateful, such as the taste of the first sip of your morning coffee, the smell of fresh rain, or the ability to use your fully functioning, healthy body. Here are three questions to end the day with.

- Who did I help today?

- What made me smile today?

- What did I learn today?

7. Bring it all together: repeat

Track your patterns for two weeks. Do you notice any trends? What did you find most challenging? What was most helpful? What surprised you? What did you learn about yourself? Acknowledge and thank yourself for doing the work. You can use any or all of these steps to help you process your feelings, find clarity and purpose, and make progress. Repeat these steps and make them a part of your routine.

Tips for coaches to use this exercise:

Encourage your clients to practice journaling to capture their thoughts, feelings, and ideas as they come up. You can help them decipher the meaning during your private sessions. You want to investigate the underlying emotion that's beneath the obvious one. Often it will take a series of questions to uncover the real issue.

Case Study

My client Dana, an operations manager, was heading towards burnout. She rarely turned down an assignment or complained about her workload. Her manager and colleagues appreciated her can-do attitude. But inside, she was mentally and emotionally exhausted. She was frustrated with the amount of work piling up, angry that people were taking advantage of her, and fearful that she might lose her job if she spoke up. By the time she got home, not only did she have little to give to her family, she often found herself lashing out at them.

Then she started using the EF Staircase tool to name and move through her emotions using the steps above. She incorporated a 15-minute walking break into her schedule to recenter every day. She left her phone back at the office and allowed herself to be fully present during her walk along a small trail. For the first few days, she was consistently experiencing emotions on the lower floors like stress, frustration, and disappointment. By reflecting on these patterns she began moving up the staircase.

Her first goal was to get curious. Whenever she noticed a stressful feeling, she started asking questions such as, "How is this task aligned with our top priorities, what resources are available to me to complete this work, what can I take off my plate, and, who can help me with this?" This helped not only shift her emotional state immediately, but over time it allowed her to communicate her needs effectively and create healthy boundaries at work.

The following week she added a daily gratitude practice on her commute home. During this exercise she asked three questions. What made me smile today? Who did I help today? The next time we spoke she was a little calmer and confident about her ability to manage through the stresses of the day.

Overcoming the Monsters that Keep us From our Dreams
By Logan Griffith

This exercise will help you understand how to fight the emotions that keep us from achieving our dreams. You will learn to detect the monster emotions that slow us down and the hero emotions that can drive them away. As you gather an army of heroes, the monsters cannot stop you anymore. You will be free to follow your dreams!

Great for:

- Those with big dreams who find themselves sabotaging their own success.

- Stopping the cycle of giving up and/or procrastinating on goals.

- Those with negative thoughts and emotions driving their life decisions.

- Feeling empowered to take action towards dreams even when challenging emotions come up.

I'll never forget my first encounter with the dream-killing monster. It all started when I learned to play basketball as a kid with my dad over the summer. Playing basketball was super fun. I was learning to dribble and practicing my shots, celebrating my wins, and being cheered on as I got better and better. A positive belief grew in me. I loved basketball and would end up being great at this game.

The summer was over, and second grade started. During recess, some older kids asked if I wanted to play and I said,

"Yes, of course." They were in fourth grade and had played for years. Almost immediately, they told me how bad I was. As the bullying continued, a new belief was born. I was and would always be horrible at basketball. After a few weeks, I gave up. When my dad asked me to play, I refused. Instead, I sat at home watching television.

My dad took me aside and asked me which thoughts made me not want to play basketball anymore. I searched deep inside and found a voice repeating over and over in my head: "I'm no good. I'm horrible at basketball. I'm not enough. I'll never be good at basketball." It was the voice of the bullies, and it made me feel so bad that I had given up on my basketball dreams. It was at this moment when I realized the voice was like a monster whispering in my ear.

All I had to do was think of basketball, and the monster would come for me. He would show up and steal my courage, motivation, and dreams. After a while, I saw monsters in other kids, too, such as the fear monster, the distraction monster, and more. All these bad feelings we kept within ourselves were like an invisible army that had one purpose: to keep us from following our dreams.

Once I realized these monsters were separate from me, I became fascinated with learning all about them. As my research progressed, I started creating strategies to fight the monsters. I was so excited to discover there were specific heroes that could fight off each monster. Since then, I have dedicated much of my life to learning and teaching the way of the Heroes and the Monsters through my Junior Mastermind.

As I shared the hero and monster concepts, it surprised me how many people saw the monsters in their lives as well. I made dozens of videos, led seminars, and taught about the monsters in my mastermind. As more and more people noticed these monsters, they joined me and used my tools to overcome their own monsters and to rise up. People who have applied the lessons in this chapter have taken control of their emotions and are now free to follow their dreams.

Monsters are the thoughts or feelings that keep us from our dreams. These monsters start tiny and grow with every limiting story we believe. Both children and adults use monsters against others to feel powerful. When they do, the monsters spread to those they attack. If a person has monsters around them for too long, they start to identify with them. Then they cannot distinguish between the monster and themselves. When bullies try to take away our light, they create monsters within us that keep us from following our dreams. If we believe these monsters and do not fight them, they stay with us, and we become discouraged even when the bullies are no longer there.

Every time we believe we don't deserve our dreams, the monsters grow stronger. After a while, we come to feel that we can no longer experience the life we want. These monsters now stay with us. They continue to whisper in our ears, taking our courage and stealing our determination. As more monsters come, they overwhelm us with fear. We stop going towards our dreams.

Monsters have an enormous influence on our lives and only one thing can save us from them. We must call on the heroes. If we call upon the right heroes, they can use the monsters' weaknesses against them. The heroes can drive these monsters away for good.

Now I'm going to teach you how to save yourselves from the monsters when they show up. I will show you how to detect when these monsters come for you, what to do when they arrive, and how to overcome them. With practice, these steps will help you get the jump on the monsters.

The first part of this strategy is to notice when these monsters arrive as quickly as possible. This is because all monsters start small, and it's much easier to fight the monsters in the beginning.

You can tell when a monster arrives by the way it makes you feel. First, you will begin to feel stress growing inside. Next, a general feeling of unease will fill your body, and it will feel like something is squeezing your heart. You can also be sure a monster has you if you find yourself hesitating, holding back, or even running from your dreams. Or if you hear discouraging whispers in your mind when you try to move forward in life.

Once you have detected the monster, it's important to figure out which monster it is. Identifying the monster is the only way to know what to do next. Below, I give just a few examples of the monsters that come for us all.

One of the most powerful monsters of all is the 'Fear Monster'. It grows larger every time someone attacks our self-belief. It grows when others say we aren't good enough and we don't deserve to be great. The fear monster might say to you, "Who are you to be great?" or "Say no to this new opportunity, it is too risky." This monster's greatest enemies are the 'Yes Hero' and the 'The Courageous Hero'.

The 'Rejection Monster' moves to reject our dreams before we can make them happen. This monster destroys the energy and courage we need to make an impact, and it keeps us from connecting with others. It might say to you, "Don't bother creating this, as it will never be good enough.", "No matter what you do, people won't accept and appreciate you." This monster's greatest enemies are the 'Self Belief Hero' and the 'Contribution Hero'.

The 'Angry Monster' blames others for our pain. It makes us act in ways we regret later. When it lashes out at others, it feeds their monsters. It might say to you, "This is not fair, there is nothing you can do, and it's their fault that you are angry!" The Angry Monster's greatest enemies are the 'Gratitude Hero' and the 'Peaceful Hero'.

The 'Sadness Monster' finds stories, people, and reasons to justify itself. It seeks to fill itself with comfort and yet can never be comforted. Instead, it paralyzes us and ignores all the dreams and greater purpose we crave. This monster might say to you, "What's the use? It won't work out and it takes too much energy. Nothing works out for you." This monster's greatest enemies are the 'Energy Hero' and the 'Happiness Hero'.

The 'Distraction Monster' thrives on immediate gratification. It will do anything to avoid purpose or pain. Often, this monster seems harmless, so we allow it to steal our dreams more readily. "You can do that later. It's very important to do this new thing now." This monster's greatest enemies are the 'The Action Hero' and the 'Focus Hero'.

Now you know a few examples of the monsters that come for us. Use the steps in the exercise below to slay these monsters one by one until you are free to go after your dreams.

Here are your steps-

1. **Go towards your dreams** - Re-focus on your dreams. What do you want? Where do you want to go? What do you want to feel? See your dream achieved as if it

has already happened. Start taking action towards your dream.

2. **Detect the monster** - Now focus on the present moment and search for any monsters stopping you or slowing you down. Ask yourself, "What thoughts or feelings are keeping me from going after my dreams right now?"

3. **Identify the monster** - Identify the monster more clearly. Which one is it? How powerful is it? What does it feel like? Who is the hero you can call on to fight this monster?

4. **Banish the monster** - Break your pattern to push this monster out of your body. You can do this by standing up, shaking yourself, and saying, or yelling, "This monster no longer has me. I am not this monster, I am free." As your presence grows, the monster will weaken.

5. **Call on the hero** - Call in your hero to protect you. What is the hero that this monster can't stand? Ask the hero to protect you. If you are distracted, call in the 'Focused Hero.' Say or yell, "I am focused, I am focused, I am focused." Identify more with your 'Focused Hero'.

6. **Create your army** - Guard the gate of your mind. Ask this hero to stay with you to keep the monster away. Call upon him any time in the future to fight for you again. Soon you will have an army of heroes waiting to fight for you.

7. **Celebrate your Victory** - Pat yourself on the back. Feel your success, as there is one hero greater than all others. You! You are the hero you have been waiting for! Now there is nothing that can stop you.

Now you have everything you need to awaken your true self. You can now detect and fight the monsters, call on the heroes and follow your dreams! Yes! Yes! Yes!

Do you want to learn more about Heroes and Monsters? Just go to http://www.heroesfightmonsters.com and get your exclusive companion worksheet for this chapter. Also, get more videos, worksheets, lessons, and resources you can use to fight the monsters that keep you from your dreams.

Beat Work Stress with this 5 Minute Technique
By Matt Adams

This exercise will help you detox from difficult emotions, create change in your life, and step into being the person you truly want to become. By installing new, positive statements within your mind, you'll be able to combat stress, release yourself from anxiety and generate positive change in every area of your life.

Great for:

- Sufferers of anxiety, stress, overwhelm, or burnout.

- Those overwhelmed with negative or unhelpful thoughts and emotions.

- Learning to manage emotions to take back control of your life.

The technique I'm about to share with you changed my life. I could even say, it saved my life.

In August 2006, at age 27, I experienced my second 'stage' of work-related stress. (The first one had been when I was 24 and suffered burnout from managing two real estate sales offices.) I was driving along a busy road in Brisbane, Australia, when I answered a call from a friend.

Within seconds of taking the call, completely out of the blue, my heart started pounding. My immediate response was to push myself back and upwards in my seat, in an effort to get it to stop somehow. I thought I was having a heart attack. I still had the steering wheel in one hand and my mobile phone in the other, and I couldn't pull over because I was driving along the Brisbane River.

The 'attack' lasted for about eight seconds. After it finished, I had a layer of perspiration over any exposed skin and the tip of my tongue was numb. Collecting myself, I thought, "What the hell was that?"

In the direction I was driving, there was a doctor's clinic only five minutes away. So I drove straight there. I told the doctor what happened and she connected me up to an ECG machine, and... nothing. No sign of anything, nothing abnormal.

It was at that moment that I linked this event to both my previous work stress a few years earlier (which had affected me for the three years leading up to this panic attack) and a current situation that could be creating stress for me. Earlier in the week I had been interviewed for a job with a leading Australian real estate website and was told they'd be getting back to me by the end of the week.

The day of the panic attack was a Thursday, around 11 a.m. I was offered the job at 2 p.m. that same day.

The following four months were the worst four months of my life. I initially accepted the job, then three days later I 'resigned', because I was due to fly to Melbourne at 6 the next morning for a week-long induction training course. The thought of being 'stuck' in an office all week without being able to 'breathe' just messed me up. It messed up my mind to the point where I thought the only way I'd survive the week ahead was to not start the job.

Four days later I was working in a factory making ladders. Seriously. I received a call from a recruitment agency that I submitted my resume to about a year earlier. Randomly, she said, "We have this position, it starts tomorrow at 2 p.m. and it's yours if you want it."

Talk about serendipity. I knew this job would suit me because I could do the work physically without having any stress on my mind. Over the next four months, I experienced up to 100 heart palpitations per day, had daily 'lightening shock' feelings in my heart, only worked an average of 4 days per week (and was almost fired), and had the thought and feeling that "I could die at any second" thousands of times.

Then one day, I was at a second hand bookshop doing my usual browsing, when one particular book caught my eye. That book changed my life. I learned about an amazing technique that allows you to reprogram your thoughts and feelings, and therefore, change your experiences.

After implementing the technique I reduced the heart palpitations to almost zero, eliminated the lightning-shock feelings completely, took just one day off work in the following 7 months, and regained the confidence/belief that I could return to my 'normal' field of work in Sales.

The technique is called The 22x11 Technique and is outlined in a book called 'Absolute Happiness' by Michael Domeyko Rowland.

Just like when you need to upgrade a software program on your computer and the system notifies you that before you can install the new version, it first has to uninstall the old version. The 22x11 technique works the same way, by uninstalling the old, negative, limiting belief, while simultaneously installing the new, positive statement of your choosing.

Some of the positive statements I've used with the 22x11 technique are:

"Work is easy and fun for me"

"My heart is calm and relaxed in perfect ways"

"My heart is strong, healthy, and happy"

"I am growing stronger and healthier every day"

Remember, the positive statement needs to be in direct opposition to your current experience, thought, feeling, or belief. The technique installs the positive statement while simultaneously uninstalling the negative 'junk' thoughts and feelings related to the statement. 'Out with the old, in with the new.' It's quite enlightening or eye-opening to see the type of junk thoughts that come up as you write down the positive statement.

Once I started using this technique, my mind came up with thoughts along the lines of *'It's killing you,'* and *'You're going to die.'* And I obviously didn't die. It's important that you don't buy into this negative junk that comes up. Just discard it like you do a bag of trash out of your house. Let it go. Trust that the positive statement is the one that's taking hold.

Some signs that the technique has worked or is working include:

- A deep sigh

- A yawn

- A physical sensation (perhaps in your brain or in your body)

- Feeling the need to sleep

These are all subtle signs that a release has happened. And that's a great thing. Mission accomplished. But make sure you continue with the technique for the full 11 days to ensure you clean out any and all junk thoughts.

I've used this technique so many times when I've literally felt like I could die at any second because of the sensations I was experiencing in my heart. This has been one of many techniques I use to create change in my mind and body, but it's my number one go-to that works the best for me.

This technique can be used to remove essentially anything 'negative' in your life. Whether it be a negative health situation, an old unwanted pattern of behavior, or if you'd simply like to install a new positive belief.

As an example, let's say you're job hunting and you have a negative belief: "I don't perform well in job interviews."

You could use the 22x11 technique by choosing a new positive belief such as: "I'm calm and confident in job interviews." That might bring up junk thoughts like: 'I'm hopeless,' 'they don't like me,' or 'you'll never get a job.' Getting this negative junk out of your subconscious mind is exactly what you want, which is why I love this technique so much.

Steps:

1. You take your current negative thought or feeling (e.g. lightning shock sensations in your heart or a thought like "*Work makes me stressed*").

2. You then come up with a positive statement that is the direct opposite of your negative thought, feeling, or belief (e.g. "*My heart is happy and healthy*" or "*Work is fun and easy*").

3. You write down the positive statement once, and say it out loud too if you like. Then underneath that, write whatever immediate thought comes to mind.

Eg. *"My heart is happy and healthy"*

Response: *"That's a lie"*

Then you repeat this process over and over, 22 times, with the format:

Positive statement

Immediate response

With the immediate responses that you write down, don't 'buy into' them in any way. Just like you don't give a second thought to the trash you take out of your house and toss into the municipal trash, don't give a second thought to the trash your mind comes back with.

With each of the 22 statements and responses, you're both installing (the positive belief) and uninstalling (the negative beliefs). Repeating it for 11 days straight simply helps with the installation and uninstalling process.

You repeat the same or different statements throughout the year if you like. As long as you're above ground, there will always be negative beliefs to uninstall from your mind... this is the life on Earth we all signed up for, so embrace it and make the best of it.

4. Then you repeat this process every day for 11 days straight. If you miss a day, the 11 days start over again from scratch.

The 22x11 technique is one of the most effective techniques for change that I've come across. I've been using it on a monthly basis for over 16 years now, and I'll continue to use it for the next 60 years.

It works for me and I'm sure it can work for you too.

Find Your True Voice: Overcome the Inner Critic and Create the Life You Want
By Donna Cookson

This exercise will aid you in recognizing, identifying, and reframing the internal, critical voice in your mind. You will learn to design your intentions and strategically craft a belief system that results in the improvements you desire in your life. You will also learn how to create a new script to master your new mindset.

Great for:

- Identifying your true voice and communicating confidently.

- Understanding the function of your inner dialogue and how it affects all aspects of life.

- Empowering yourself with tools to effect positive change.

- Developing a practice of positive self-talk and creating transformational personal growth.

For many years now, I have been the President of Dale Carnegie Training in Northern California. In that capacity, I have served as an expert voice on a multitude of subjects. From human relations classes, leadership development, sales training, and the big daddy of them all, the one thing that Dale Carnegie is most known for, public speaking mastery.

I've had the privilege of watching eager participants join classes in nervous anticipation, hopeful that we will magically endow them with special powers of communicating and gift them with the confidence to face any situation. And in a grueling two-day immersive program they are given the training, coaching, skills, and tools to transform themselves into a masterful, impactful communicator.

If you know anything about the legendary man, you know that Dale Carnegie was the pioneer of personal development, the man on whose shoulders folks like Tony Robbins stand. Dale Carnegie developed a legacy-producing program that has been leading the public speaking industry for more than one hundred years. He studied people for twenty years to develop his processes and expertise. It was the fact that he paid close attention to the needs of the people in his classes, dug deeper into what they were trying to accomplish, that gave him the insight and understanding that ultimately enabled him to crack the code of personal development.

And yet, as I watched over the years the thousands of clients that joined the prestigious club of Carnegie graduates, I couldn't help but notice that they all had something in common. They were willing to part with thousands of dollars in order to tame the inner critic and finally feel like they belonged on stage. It was this voice that taunted them into believing they weren't good enough, confident enough, or worthy enough to express themselves in a meaningful and eloquent way.

As sure as I am that we can provide course participants with technical skills, practice, tools, tips, and tricks that will have them performing at incredible levels, I couldn't help but wonder about how we could, as coaches, help people find their *true* inner voice – the one beyond their critical self-judgments. The truth about overcoming a fear of public speaking (or any other fear for that matter) is convincing yourself you can do it. And therein lies the issue: what we believe about ourselves is what we believe about ourselves.

Could it be that simple? I understand that a lot of unique details go into the delicate psyche of each of us. We are made up of our experiences, our traumas, our memories. We're shaped by the myriad of people that have influenced us. However, if we could boil all our anxieties down to a simple problem, it might be this: our inner voice can either drive us to success or doom us to failure. Sometimes seemingly without our buy-in.

Many of us feel held hostage by that little voice, deep in the quiet recesses of our mind. The voice that replays old recordings from traumatic events, cruel people who spoke doubt into our hearts, and even self-hatred that permeates our thoughts and actions. That voice replays old recordings that tell us we are limited, lacking, and unable. Perhaps it makes bold declarations of our unworthiness and taunts us with reminders of the bad things we may have thought, said, or done to others. It is the keeper of records of wrongdoing, limitations, insecurities, and every fear of inadequacy we ever imagined.

My personal story weaves a tapestry of interesting skills, experiences, education, and opportunity. So many life lessons I've learned have pointed me to the path I stand on now. I've faced demons, heartbreaks, and losses with the best of them. And in the end, what I finally figured out is that it was my own thought process that determined my outcomes.

Let's go back to a previous time in my life. About fifteen years ago, long before my time at Dale Carnegie, I went through a complete life reset. I went through a difficult divorce, major surgery, financial insecurity, returning to college to complete my degree, and becoming a single parent of three teenagers. It was the first time I'd been on my own, and I began to seek out understanding from any source I could find that would help me to overcome my fears and finally achieve the greatness I had secretly believed dwelled inside me. I remembered having thoughts about myself as a little girl of feeling that I was meant for greatness. It was just a kernel of thought at the time and I quickly tucked it away. Later, it became buried deep beneath the confusion of a dysfunctional family life, traumatic abuses, and a complete lack of self-worth that would take many years to unravel.

During this reset, I persevered and pursued knowledge, insight, and pearls of wisdom from college, certifications, seminars, therapy, coaching, and any other source I could find to teach me how to unbelieve wrong things and to cling to beautiful beliefs about myself, my abilities and my future.

I've taken all the things I've learned about creating a magnificent inner voice and I'd like to share it here with you. You can choose at any time to believe something different, to make a change, to bravely take a new path. It sounds simple, but I believe it's a truly magical formula!

Here are seven steps to overcome your inner critic and create the life you want:

Step 1: Identify the critical inner voice and write down what it is telling you

Acknowledge that the thoughts from your inner critic are different from your conscious perspective. Our unconscious limiting beliefs can be in direct conflict with our conscious thoughts. Some of these thoughts might be "I'm not good enough," "I can't do anything right," etc. Get quiet and write them all down in the third person voice, such as "You can't do anything right!"

Remember that your critical inner voice is not necessarily reflecting reality. It's just coming up with thoughts you adopted based on destructive early life experiences and attitudes directed toward you from other people that you've internalized.

Step 2: Take the time to identify the difference between your Conscious Mind (CM) and Unconscious Mind (UM):

CM is the part of you that is verbal, thinking, logical, rational, & conceptualizes things	UM is non-verbal, feeling, spatial, & is beyond language
CM is only aware of *now*	UM stores & controls your memories, is aware of your past & future. (It's like an audio recorder that's been recording since the beginning of your time)
CM learns sequentially – one after another	UM learns concurrently (can learn multiple things at the same time)
CM needs time to learn something	UM can learn instantaneously, & is experiential
CM is in charge of voluntary movements	UM is in charge of involuntary movements
CM is thinking	UM is feeling
CM is the goal *setter*	UM is the goal-*getter*
CM asks questions like *why?*	UM already knows the answer
CM tries to understand the problem	UM already knows the solution

Remember that the goal is to have your Conscious Mind and your Unconscious Mind integrate with one another. That means that there is an internal alignment of beliefs. This can be achieved by asking yourself what the higher purpose is for each belief. For instance, the higher purpose for being defensive might be to protect yourself because you seek security. When you can understand that both sides (CM/UM) are coming from a place that seeks your higher good, they can become integrated and your beliefs will be congruent.

Step 3: Create a response to the limiting thoughts you wrote previously.

You can respond to your inner critic by writing down a more realistic and compassionate evaluation of yourself. Write the responses in the first person (as "I" statements). In response to a thought like, "You're such an idiot," you could write: "I may struggle at times, but I am smart and competent in many ways."

Step 4: The important thing to do now is to *reframe* your thoughts and determine what you want.

Instead of being lazy, you might want to be energetic. Instead of calling yourself stupid, you want to be smart and capable! This is an important step; you cannot skip this. You must be able to say it like you want it! Take the time to get clear on what you want instead of the negative thought.

Step 5: Remember that the Unconscious Mind is a *goal-getter*.

It is responding to perceived directives when it hears statements. It could be creating situations that are keeping you from moving forward because of these confusing messages. Practice "feeding" your UM questions to keep it "busy" pursuing goals. Our UM responds well to "Why" and "How" sentences. Write as many questions as you can think of that have positive language and give your UM something to work on. For example, "Why am I attracting a great opportunity for advancement at work?", "How is it that I'm in optimal health?", or "Why do I feel happy, healthy, and excited about my future?"

Step 6: Create a vision for yourself.

Imagine your life 1, 5, or 10 years from now. Visualize it and write it down. Go into detail about the sounds, sights, tastes, feelings, smells, and thoughts you have as you are in your ideal setting. The more detail you can give the picture, the better. Once you have the vision written down, begin to make a separate list of the qualities and traits you will have in your vision. Then begin to form questions around having those traits and qualities.

Step 7: Train yourself to be in charge of your UM by creating the questions and goals it pursues.

For example, "Why do I offer myself great care and love at all times?", "How is it that I'm attracting new friends who are like-minded, supportive and loyal?" or "Why do I attract wealth and find new ways to increase my income?"

Make these steps a regular practice and watch your life transform into the vision you've designed.

PART 2
ENERGY MEDICINE:

HEAL YOUR BODY,
MIND & SPIRIT

Heaven Rushing In: Receive Divine Energies for Support and Inspiration
By Rachel Jacobson

This exercise can change your day in an instant. It can nudge or propel you into action and lift your emotional state. It's a simple, short exercise that you can use anytime you're feeling stuck, unmotivated, or uninspired. Move forward in life with more ease, clarity, and momentum.

Great for:

- Those who experience low mood, depression, and/or overwhelm.

- Those who struggle to make decisions and feel lost, confused, or stuck.

- Those with a physical or emotional issue that's ongoing and unresolved.

- Those who keep procrastinating and would like to feel more motivated and inspired.

I've often heard it said that life is a journey, not a destination. Along the way, life can get incredibly complex, and it can be difficult to know how to navigate the daily throes of a busy, fast-paced world, while at the same time being a human with a physical body and a wide range of emotions.

That's why I think it's profound and magnificent when we find simple, fast actions we can take that have a positive impact on our quality of life and our ability to thrive, rather than just survive. This Eden Method energy medicine exercise (created by Donna Eden) called Heaven Rushing In, can shift your energies from a state of stuckness and inertia to feeling inspired to create the life you want. Consider how powerful it would be if you always felt you knew what your next action or step should be. What if it was easy for you to take that step? How would your life change if you always felt able to move forward on your journey?

When I was a teenager, I experienced years of depression, anxiety, and an eating disorder. I tried many therapies and found energy medicine to be a game-changer. When I began to learn about energy and how I could balance my own energies, everything changed.

I used to spend hours in bed, curled up under the covers, unable to face the day. Life was a rollercoaster of emotions and I often felt stuck and unmotivated. I also used to feel very alone and unsupported. So, it was a beautiful surprise and relief to discover that I wasn't destined for a lifetime of misery and challenges and that there were exercises I could do, with my own hands, to help myself feel better.

Our main energy systems (meridians, chakras, aura, etc.) are extraordinarily intricate. Both minor and major energy disruptions to these systems push us out of balance, but even small shifts in how we interact with our energy can create positive impacts on our well-being. In the years I've been using energy exercises to relieve my symptoms, I've realized that, instead of pushing or expecting myself to make big changes, I could first tap into the divine well of support and wisdom from "the heavens."

I began using this exercise frequently to both access my inner wisdom and utilize these outer channels of universal energies for my healing. I no longer felt as if I didn't have any answers. No matter what challenges life was throwing my way, I had a way of resourcing outside support and guidance. This has led me to feel empowered and able to move through life with more ease. And it doesn't always need to take a long time to make a change. Within a few short minutes, I could make a small but meaningful difference in my emotions and actions.

This exercise helps to open your mind, heart, and energy field so that you can receive these supportive energies available to you. It's your choice how you perceive them. Although it helps you receive divine energies from "the heavens," you could also say energy from "the universe," information from "source," information from your higher self, or personal wisdom.

Here are the steps for this beautiful energy medicine exercise that's gentle and easy for anyone to do.

Steps:

1. Stand with your feet shoulder-width apart (or, if you need, modify it to be seated or lying down).

2. Rub the palms of your hands together for several seconds, then place your palms facing down at the top of each of your legs.

3. Inhale and bring your hands together in a prayerful position, with your palms touching in front of your chest. Hold for a few seconds and exhale.

4. Inhale and reach both of your arms up over your head, with your arms open to the sides and your palms facing up. In this position, you are opening to the divine energies above from "the heavens."

5. Exhale and hold this position, allowing yourself to breathe naturally and welcome in lots of divine energies.

6. Hold this position for as long as you'd like, then slowly lower your arms, as if you're cradling the air around you, bringing your hands to rest on your heart.

Tips for applying this exercise:

It's fantastic to do this exercise outdoors because you can connect to the divine energies in a way that's almost as if you're touching the sky. You also get the grounding, calming benefits of being out in nature. But this exercise will work in any location. You can also do the exercise in a seated position or lying down.

If you feel you'd benefit from receiving more of these divine energies (extra support, motivation, and inspiration) then once you have completed the exercise one time, repeat steps 4-6 as many times as you'd like.

Extend the exercise into your personal meditative process

Combine any of the suggestions below to create your own meditative process.

You can hold the open-armed position at steps 4 and 5 for a longer amount of time. This is often a powerful, meditative process. If you take this approach, be kind to your body and support your arms with cushions or pillows. Try lying down in a fully relaxed position, combining the exercise with music, a guided meditation, or other ways to create a calm, soft and soothing ambiance, such as diffusing essential oils or lighting a candle. When you open your arms to receive the divine energies, you may prefer to have your arms outstretched by your sides with your palms facing up. Whether you choose to have your arms by your sides or over your head, I recommend using cushions or pillows to support them. You'll be able to stay in the position for a long time and benefit from an abundance of divine energies rushing into your palms and then carried into your heart.

If you have a question about an area of concern or uncertainty in your life, you can ask it when you do the exercise. Let's say you're feeling unsure about whether to accept a new job and would like divine guidance to help you decide. When you open your arms to the divine energies, think about the new job possibility and ask a question such as, "What would be useful for me to know or understand?" or "What would be for the greatest good?" Of course, you can formulate any question you'd like.

This exercise is also brilliant for setting intentions, then receiving energy that supports you in fulfilling your intention. An example of this could be drinking a certain amount of water. If you've decided to make this type of lifestyle change, it can be tricky to implement the change with ease. Make it easy for yourself by resourcing the divine energy outside of you. In this example, as you do step 3 of the exercise, you would think, sense, trust or ask that the energies you receive in steps 4 and 5 will support you in carrying out your intention of drinking more water. Then, while you do steps 4 and 5, continue to think, sense, trust and know that the energies you're receiving are supporting you with your intention.

Another great way to use this exercise is when you're beginning a project or have a long list of tasks ahead. When you want to get started and take the first step, but you're struggling to feel motivated or generate momentum, do this exercise.

Tips for coaches:

Ask your client to do this exercise before they embark on another coaching activity or healing session. When clients are about to enter a process of self-reflection, growth, and change, it can help to set the stage by doing this exercise. Your client will drop into a more centered, embodied place where they have more connection to the wisdom of the heavens and their own heart. This is particularly helpful with clients who spend a lot of time living in their heads and tend to get overwhelmed with overthinking.

You can also use this exercise for integration. If a client has experienced a shift in their energies or a change in mindset, it's often valuable to close your session with Heaven Rushing In. This cultivates further insights for your client that support their overall healing and integration of divine energies with their own energies, body, mind, and spirit.

Intuitive Grounding: A Method to Calm Yourself and Come Home to Your Body
By Halley Claire Bass

Grounding is a practice that will help you to release frenetic energy in your body, mind, and spirit. You'll learn how to develop a deeper connection with the supportive energy of Mother Earth, and use that connection to help you stay calm, focused, and feel more at ease with yourself, people around you, and your life as a whole.

Great for:

- People who are struggling with anxiety, overwhelm, nervousness, or low confidence

- Empaths and highly sensitive people who often take on the energy and thoughts of others around them

- Overthinkers and over-analyzers who want to become more fully present in their body

- Busy people who need a quick practice to feel calm and in the moment

---

When I first learned about intuitive grounding, it changed my life. I hadn't known I could intentionally direct the current of my energy to be supportive and healing for my body, spirit, and soul. It was the first time I could actually meditate and quiet my mind when other methods didn't work for me.

My first experience with grounding was in Berkeley, California circa 2010. I walked into a spiritual shop and met an energy healer. Straight away, she noticed I was ungrounded. She could tell that I was living a lot from my thoughts and mind and that I wasn't completely present.

As an Aquarius, who is often in my head and thinking about ideas, I spend a lot of my time daydreaming in the clouds; my spirit freely wandering around in the realm of ideas, dreams, and pictures. Many of us walk around completely unaware of our energetic bodies because we live in a society that values the mind much more than the body and the spirit.

The healer taught me how to ground myself, and something clicked for me. I realized that all this time I was directing my energy upward. This is what allowed me to have such positive spiritual experiences and what gave me such a strong gift of being a visionary, someone who visualizes everything, and sees what is beyond the surface. What I hadn't realized is that I needed more support to move my energy downward so that I could feel more in my body, and enjoy more of my life.

The downward motion of energy in our bodies creates a calming and healing place to feel safe and connected to life here on Earth. If you are lacking self-esteem, struggling to reach your goals, feeling anxious or worried, or everything just feels difficult, it may be the case that you need to ground your energy.

Frenetic energy in the body can be caused by a lot of factors. If you are highly sensitive or very empathic, your body is easily carrying around a lot of other people's energy. You may feel lost or disconnected from life, or sometimes feel so overwhelmed you want to float away.

That's where intuitive grounding comes in. It is the very first intuitive medicine tool because it takes our awareness inward and creates an immediate connection to the loving, healing, supporting energy of Mother Earth. Before we can tap into our deeper intuition, we must be fully present in our bodies to sense and feel what is coming through.

Although we won't go into the chakras (energy centers of the body) in this exercise, it may be useful to know that your tailbone is the location of your root chakra, the energetic center that is spiritually connected to your sense of safety, taking up space in life, and how you relate to the people in your family tree. If you have challenges with any of these, as most of us do, intuitive grounding is a wonderful exercise to support your healing journey on an energetic level.

With so much information happening in the mind through-out our days, we often forget the importance of the work our energy body is doing. So take a moment to pause, ground, and feel your deep, intimate connection with your body and with Mother Earth.

Steps:

The very first time you connect with your intuitive ground-ing energy, you will want to be in a quiet, meditative place. The more you do this practice, however, the easier it will become to quickly access this energetic grounding wherever you are.

1. Begin with placing your feet firmly on the ground and lengthening your spine. Feel the weight of your body on the chair below you, and the ground pushing up against your feet. This is your first step in noticing the gravita-tional pull, the natural energetic symbiosis that we have between the Earth and our bodies.

2. Close your eyes and take a few deep breaths. Allow your lungs to expand a little bit more each time you inhale, and each time you exhale see if you can let all of the air out. As you begin to deepen your breath and connect with this natural rhythm of the body, allow your focus to turn inward.

3. With this inward attention, find your tailbone at the base of your spine. See if you can give it a little wiggle, and say hello to your tailbone. Thank your tailbone for existing and for all the work that it does. This way, you begin to develop a loving relationship with a part of your body you don't often interact with.

4. Now, imagine an energetic cord that roots from the base of your spine and travels down to the Earth. You may imagine this cord as a rope with an anchor, a cascade of diamonds, a beam of light, a chain, or whatever comes to your imagination. When working with intuitive healing, your imagination is your source of wisdom. Allow your creative imagination to visualize the grounding cord however you like.

5. Now that you have pictured the grounding cord in your mind's eye, picture it traveling down from the base of your spine through all the layers of the earth. Imagine that it is going deep down, through each layer of soil and lava until it reaches the core of the Earth. Visualize a rock with your name on it, at the center of the earth. Imagine your cord wrapping around that rock, solidifying your grounding. If you'd like, you can imagine that roots are growing outward, across all corners of the Earth, deeper and wider, to strengthen the base of this energetic grounding.

6. Begin to notice how you feel now that you have set your intuitive grounding. Take a few deep breaths here and just allow yourself to notice the feeling.

7. Once you are tethered to the Earth with your energetic grounding cord, you can take the next process of releasing any unwanted energy out of the cord and into the Earth. If something is plaguing you or if you have a sensation in the body, visualize the energy rolling up into a ball of light, and traveling down your grounding cord out of the body. Imagine that whatever you are letting go of can travel down the cord, getting sucked out like a vacuum to be composted away into the energetic circuit board of the Earth.

8. The last step in this practice is to receive the loving and supportive energy of Mother Earth. To do this, place your awareness at the bottom of your feet. Imagine a color that makes you think of the earth, and visualize a ball of energy coming from the Earth and circulating through your legs and then back down the grounding cord.

This circulating Earth energy provides you with extra stability, support, and a loving presence in your body. As you allow the Earth's energy to circulate up your feet, through your legs, and back down your grounding cord, start to notice how it feels. What new sensations are arising?

When you get the hang of it, you can let go of the picture and trust that the energy will continue to circulate as you need it. Sit for a few more quiet minutes to allow your nervous system to synchronize with the slow and steady rhythm of the Earth's pulse.

When you feel a bit more at ease you can give yourself a big hug, thank yourself for taking a few minutes out of your day for this self-care practice, and thank Mother Earth for her care and support, before opening your eyes and interacting again with the outside world.

The ideal scenario is that you practice with intuitive grounding so often that you can do it quickly and on-demand when you are feeling off. The more you practice, the more confident you will become.

It is especially ideal for anyone who is holding space for another human - such as coaches, counselors, or healers - to use this practice before working with clients. It allows you to feel more present and connected with yourself so that you can be there for the person who needs you.

Now that you have an intuitive grounding practice, you can ground yourself and reach out for the loving, healing support of Mother Earth, anytime you need.

Tips for coaches:

If your client is feeling anxious, too in their head, or feeling overwhelmed by difficult emotions, you can guide them through this practice. Start by just doing the energetic grounding cord visualization, so that they don't feel overwhelmed by every step. Then you can add on the releasing energy and the circulating of earth energy the second or third time you practice with this exercise.

Give your clients time to get into their grounding. Encourage them to use their imagination, and to not hold back whatever they see. You can support your client with their grounding, by asking them what they see or feel, and also visualizing it with them.

Either during or upon completing the meditation, you can ask your client to share about the experience, how it felt, and what it was like. Be sure to not rush through the process, giving them time to feel the support of Earth energy.

Upon completion of the meditation, I encourage you to guide the client to give themselves a big hug of gratitude, for showing up with curiosity and imagination in this practice of reconnecting to this really strong and powerful self-healing tool.

The Sadhana of Food: Practicing the Art of Sacred Eating
By Satyavani Gayatri

The way you eat your food has a huge impact on your physical, mental-emotional, and spiritual health. This chapter offers a daily ritual for preparing, eating, and cleaning up afterward to help you develop a sacred relationship with food and transform eating meals into a daily spiritual practice.

Great for:

- Those experiencing digestive problems or having trouble maintaining a healthy weight.

- Strengthening your immune system.

- Increasing and maintaining energy throughout the day.

- Those suffering from anxiety, excessive stress, and/or disturbed sleep.

- Cultivating a daily spiritual practice and building a more conscious and expansive life.

The sacred ritual of eating is a lost practice in today's world. We have given up the process of giving thanks and recognizing nourishment as a spiritual act for food-like substances that are fast and cheap with little attention to the physical, mental, emotional, and spiritual implications it has on our bodies and minds. Sadhana, the practice of performing a devotional act, of making something sacred, is an easy process that can be applied to our daily food consumption as well as to our daily regimen. This simple ritual has a profound impact on our digestive health, mental-emotional health, and spiritual development.

The *sadhana of food* is more than a practice of slowing down so we can taste our food better – it is an intimate process of creating space for greater focus and expansive awareness. It is the celebration of the divinity within, that is housed within our physical bodies. Yes, on the superficial level, the act of consumption facilitates the biochemical process of transforming food into energy so we can move, heal and stay active in our day-to-day lives. But what it also does is expand our consciousness so we become more aware of all the types of 'food' we are taking into our being. It helps us build our sacred selves.

From an Ayurvedic and spiritual perspective, food is more than fruits, vegetables, nuts, seeds, dairy, and the like. Food is any type of energy we choose to take into our consciousness that directly impacts our multi-layered self. It is often said in both Ayurvedic and spiritual teachings that *food begins in the mind and our environment.* What are we taking in as 'nourishment' from the outside world and what impact does that have on our health? When we examine the ritual of food in this way we gain a different perspective on what it means to be truly healthy.

Before my studies at the Kripalu Center, I had a very complicated relationship with food. Having suffered from an eating disorder and body dysmorphia for over two decades prior, I read and self-facilitated every type of diet and nutritional plan imaginable looking for the one perfect diet. As my spiritual and Ayurvedic studies deepened in my late twenties, I rapidly began to understand that it was not the food itself that was causing my never-ending challenges, but rather my lack of mental-emotional awareness and the type of 'food' I was taking in. I lived a high-stress, fast-paced life that was unsustainable but I believed if I just kept going, everything would fall into place. Yeah, not so much.

Several years later, when studying at the Kripalu Center, I remember reading the teachings of Bapuji (Swami Kripalu) and stumbling across a quote from him regarding food: "Wisdom stays alive when excess food is absent." It was at that moment that my relationship with food transformed from eating into sadhana; a practice. I became acutely aware that all the food in my life that I agreed to take in was heightening my stress, causing incredible distraction, and pushing me into deeper and deeper states of dis-ease. My physical body was a mess and my mental-emotional state was foggy and distorted. I was exhausted, depressed, and very angry. I was not living, I was dying.

I then took it upon myself to recreate my relationship with food by experimenting with a new way of being, a spiritual way. This spiritual way was not just about the nourishment I put into my mouth but also - and more importantly - about the people, things, and places I was allowing into my life. Now that was interesting. I examined the various relationships I had, the clients I accepted, the movies I watched, the places I dined in, the music I listened to, the books I read, the environment I lived in, and the conversations I engaged in. I climbed into every aspect of my life to determine whether or not this 'food' was providing me with nourishment or if it is what I considered 'dead food.'

So, this exercise, *the sadhana of food*, can not only be applied to what you put in your bowl or on your plate but also in every aspect of your life. Are you being nourished?

Use these 10 easy steps to create a food sadhana practice:

1. Prior to preparing food, take a few moments of meditation to calm the mind and check in with your body. You can ask yourself questions to drop into a deeper state of awareness like: Am I physically hungry or am I mentally hungry? How am I feeling right now? What is the energy around me like?

2. Choose foods that are organic in nature, colorful, washed, and mostly come from the plant kingdom. These are considered *sattvic foods:* those that contain lightness, goodness, and purity. These foods will nourish you most fully, maximize your digestion, and increase your ability to sleep soundly. Processed foods only increase digestive distress, cause blood sugar fluctuations, and provide no nutritional value.

3. While preparing food, say a silent prayer or chant a mantra softly. Every spiritual tradition has one so choose what resonates with you. This cultivates openness, expansiveness, clarity, and divinity. This energy will be infused into the food that is being prepared. Remember *an unhappy cook produces unhappy food. A joyful cook produces joyful food.*

4. As the food cooks, prepare your place of nourishment (the kitchen table, the dining room, or on the floor at a small table) with reverence and thoughtfulness. Make sure that the space is clean and free of clutter. Having a space that is free of debris or disorganization allows for the food to provide maximum aroma, potency, and expansiveness.

5. Once the food is cooked, place it on clean dishware in a colorful fashion. The more colors you include in your meal, the more energetic vibration it gives off. A plate with mostly brown colors represents 'dead food' whereas a plate that displays all the colors of the rainbow has vibrancy, potency, and joy.

6. Before getting ready to consume your food, take a moment to look at what is on your plate. Notice the colors, think about all those that participated in getting it to your home – the farmers who cultivated the land and planted it, the workers that transported it, and the market clerks that displayed it for you to see and purchase. Give thanks for all that went into the process of you being able to enjoy it.

7. Upon eating, maximize your digestion by chewing each bite slowly and mindfully. In Ayurveda, it is said that chewing your food thirty-two times before swallowing will maximize your digestion and cause significantly less distress. Do not drink liquid at the same time as eating, wait until you have finished your meal to have your beverage. After each bite of food, pause by putting your spoon or fork down so you can determine when you feel full. In both Ayurvedic and spiritual practices, we adhere to the 75/25 rule. Eat until you are 75% full so that the remaining 25% can begin the process of digestion.

8. While eating, remain silent. Limit talking. Refrain from watching television or listening to loud music so you can fully focus on the eating process and not be distracted or disturbed by what you see or hear.

9. Upon completion of your meal, before transitioning to your next activity take 10-15 minutes to lay down on

your left side (the side of the descending colon) to encourage the digestive process.

10. After your brief rest, wash all of the dishes and put any remaining food or debris away so the cooking space is clean and refreshed before the next meal preparation time.

Tips for coaches that want to use this with a client:

Tell your client to start this process with only one meal per day. Many clients will get overwhelmed if they believe this has to be done for every meal in order for them to benefit from the exercise – that is not true. Health and spiritual practices are a process of building – doing one thing at a time until it becomes a positive habit and then adding on a little more. Food sadhana is a very intimate ritual that will be a different experience for each person so let your client know that this is something that they can take their time with. In addition, clients should be encouraged to make this ritual their own and even include other members of the household in it to encourage a sense of connection and community with everyone. If the client chooses to make it an individual practice that is perfectly fine, but let them know that others are welcome to join in.

It is important as a coach to be aware that this activity may bring up emotional triggers for clients in the area of food relationships, spiritual practices, or lifestyle choices. This is a great opportunity to work with your client through such challenges to help them bring to the surface their deeper thoughts and concerns. I would not be concerned if this happens as it is an opportunity for growth for your client. Let them express and explore what they may be experiencing. Remind your client that what is coming up is doing so to come out. Such releases are part of the spiritual path.

Learning to Discern: A Practice for Living in Love
By Anahata Roach

Fear causes most of the problems in the world today. Learning to listen to the still, small voice of spirit, soul, higher self, guides, God/Goddess, or whatever you call the vibration of love, is the path to a happier, less stressful life. This is a real tool anyone can use to move out of the vibration of fear as a way of life.

Great for:

- Overcoming fears that contribute to depression, anxiety, and overwhelm.

- Those stuck in abusive relationships but unable to leave them.

- Those wanting to experiment with using gratitude to develop greater presence and calmness.

- Developing a spiritual practice for overcoming the ego and embodying the soul.

As souls embodied in physical vessels, we enter this world with the freedom to choose how we live out our experience on Earth. The two choices we have are to live from a place of fear or of love. Fear comes from our ego, which always wants to keep our bodies safe and comfortable. Love is the vibration of our soul, which is the eternal frequency of universal Oneness.

Fear is a dense, visceral energy. It hangs around and weighs you down. It keeps you locked in a place of distrust, disharmony, and disease. But it is so *easy* to vibrate with! We are surrounded by fear everywhere we turn – the media in all its forms uses fear because it drives up ratings. Marketing campaigns are fear-based, appealing to the worst-case scenario on any topic because fear sells. Politicians play on exaggerated or misleading information and use fear to get elected. It truly is everywhere.

Learning to uncouple from the vibration of fear is difficult because its frequency and programming are embedded in all of us from conception.

Disclaimer: not *all* fear is bad! Fear can keep us out of danger and out of risky situations. Fear told our Neanderthal ancestors to run from the saber-toothed tiger. The reptilian part of the brain responds to fear with adrenaline and cortisol, yet neither one of these hormones is good for the body long-term.

In my client work, I see fear causing most of the problems in the world today. Fear of letting go causes depression. Fear of the future causes anxiety. Fear of change causes people to stay in abusive relationships or feel completely overwhelmed. Fear of a potentially fatal disease often seems to manifest it.

Learning to listen to the still, small voice of spirit, soul, higher self, guides, God/Goddess, or whatever you call the vibration of love, is the path to a happier, less stressful life. This isn't from a Pollyanna perspective. This is a real tool anyone can use to move out of the vibration of fear as a way of life.

Love is eternal but in the physical realm, ephemeral. Love is an intake of breath. Love is an exhale. Love is a perfect sunset or sunrise. The vibration of love is the frequency of creation. It is uplifting and joyous. It has a positive effect on your thoughts and your reality. But, it is hard to hold onto for any length of time. However, when you practice holding love in your heart and allowing it to radiate from your body, living in a state of love becomes easier and easier.

Practicing Living in Love

Realigning neural pathways to perceive life from a place of gratitude, not disillusionment, isn't as much a linear process as it is a practice. By shifting your attitude trajectory, even by 1%, you will arrive at a completely different destination.

I have personally experienced this kind of shift in a profound way. Normally, I try to walk in the park near my home several times a week. After practicing gratitude for a few days, I went for a walk through the park and felt a connection to the trees I had never sensed before. In fact, it felt to me that the entire landscape was suddenly more alive and beautiful than I had ever experienced it to be. I thought to myself, "Wow! The trees look so much more alive today!" To which the trees answered, "No sister, *you* are more alive today!"

When your energy field begins to shift to the higher frequency of love, the most amazing things happen – strangers greet you with a smile, open doors, stop their car to let you merge into traffic, a store clerk goes the extra mile to help you, on the way to an appointment you encounter more green traffic lights than red… the list goes on. Try it!

Steps to Holding the Love Frequency:

1. Journal with Gratitude

To begin, you will need a journal and pen to track at least three things you recognize as blessings throughout your day. This can be an evening ritual before bedtime or a morning ritual upon awakening. I believe that the actual act of writing on paper helps to embed the energy of gratitude in a way that typing into a laptop or phone does not. But if that is all that is available to you, go for it.

It is the *consistent* practice of gratitude that elevates your perspective to 'glass-half-full' and opens the portal to joy. Then, when life inevitably goes awry and you are feeling down, all you have to do is go back and read a few pages of your previous gratitudes to help chase away the blues.

2. Use Discernment

While you are practicing daily gratitude, you become more aware of the 'shoulds' and the mean talk you are hearing from inside your own head. Why do we let the 'inner critic' boss us around so much? In its vigilance to keep the status quo, the ego perceives any new perspective or action you consider as a threat, and you receive a verbal dressing down. For example, have you ever considered a new hairstyle and immediately hear a voice telling you how stupid that idea is, or how ridiculous you would look afterward?

Start filtering what you are receiving through the lens of discernment: Is this coming from a place of fear or love? If it is an obvious answer of fear, let it go. Spirit speaks to us lovingly and quietly, and always with an awareness that you have a choice. Spirit issues no edicts, so listening to that voice takes practice.

3. Ask to Receive

The ego loves to volunteer its opinion on everything. Spirit knows you have free will and cannot make recommendations unless asked. We often overlook that simple fact and expect to receive random instructions from the Divine. That won't happen until you humbly ask for help and guidance. When we finally surrender our need to find the answer ourselves, we receive exactly what we need.

4. Stay Present

Fear lurks in the past or projects into the future. Only when we are grounded and present in our bodies can we see or be open to the opportunities that appear before us. When was the last time you were rushing around, late for an appointment when you left something critical behind and had to go back in to get it, or tripped and fell on the way to the car, or spilled coffee onto your new clothes, all because you were focused on the future and afraid of being late? When we are present, we are in our bodies and not in our heads.

Tips for using it with a client:

When you notice recurring phrases and themes of fear-based beliefs from your client, you can gently begin to introduce this practice as a way to shift the focus from a negative perspective to a more positive one. This blends beautifully with emotional clearing work, as a way to integrate the new, freer space for self-expression.

Supporting Minerals: Crystals and stones have been used as healing talismans since humans first walked the planet. If you work with the frequencies of crystals and minerals, here are a few stones that I have found to support shifting attitudes and perspectives from a glass-half-empty perspective to half-full. Introduce and have your client work with one at a time, according to their needs. The stones can be used in meditation, carried in a pocket, or worn as jewelry.

- Hematite – an earthly, grounding energy that helps to 'be here now.'

- Aquamarine – supports the emotional body to help release old programming and perspectives.

- Black Tourmaline – helps transmute negativity to clear light.

- Bumblebee Jasper – the 'don't worry, be happy' stone that gives an optimistic vibe.

- Amethyst – brings a deep sense of divine connection and protection.

- Moldavite – has an intense energy that pushes one to transform.

A dedicated commitment to this discernment practice yields an expanded, more joyful perception and experience of life in all its facets.

A New Normal: Achieving Mastery of Oneness by Absorbing Nature Through Your Senses
By Yasheeka Divine

If you're living a fast-paced life or struggling with stress, anxiety, or depression, this chapter will help you slow down and find your inner calm. By connecting with nature through all your senses and discovering the feeling of Oneness, you'll gain access to a sustainable and healthy source of stress relief.

Great for:

- Those struggling with daily stress, anxiety, or depression.

- Those constantly living in a technological world (computers, video games, cell phones, etc).

- Those in need of a mental detox from society and day-to-day demands.

- Creating more happiness and peace.

There is a spiritual notion that *everything* which exists is connected, and that our feeling of being separate from other people and our environment is simply an illusion. When we experience Oneness, we feel a direct connection that links us to the natural world.

The primary objective of this exercise is to create an awareness that everything exists as one. Whether you have a calendar-filled schedule or lots of spare time, this exercise is meant to encourage you to make some kind of connection with nature, no matter what environment you're in. Using all of your senses, you will be guided through steps to help you visualize and reflect upon your experience and how it makes you feel. After this exercise, you will feel refreshed with a clear mind, improved respiratory and mental health, and relief from stress, depression, and anxiety.

I used to live a very busy, calendar-filled, always-on-the-go type of lifestyle. It was hard for me to schedule time to slow down. Many phases of my life were spent in the heart of busy cities in New Jersey and New York. When I lost my only child through hospital negligence, the stress from the pain and struggles of that loss had me thinking that my life was over. One day I asked myself, "How can I practice feeling whole again?" The answer I got was: nature.

Nature has always made me happy. Although I've lived close to a few parks and patches of nature where I could escape to unwind from my daily activities, I often didn't use these opportunities. I tended to just flow with the fast-paced tempo of city life, neglecting my own need to unwind and let go of emotional pain and stress.

It was only when I was grieving the loss of my child that I began to lean into nature's ability to be a catalyst for healing. One of the ways I was able to combat the negative impact of this pain and the stress of my hectic, sensory-overloaded life was to simply spend time in nature, through a concept called Forest Therapy (also known as Forest Bathing.)

Forest bathing is not a common activity for people living in metropolitan areas. According to a study sponsored by the Environmental Protection Agency, the average American spends roughly 93% of his or her time indoors. Bathing refers to immersion in a natural environment. The purpose here is to create a practice for wellness and healing through direct interaction with nature. Unfortunately, many people associate being in nature with 'roughing it.' The intention of forest bathing is to go outside to relax with nature, and in return, allow nature to help you heal holistically and naturally.

Along with reconnecting almost daily with nature, in order to de-stress we must be intentional with our breathing. Breathing in oxygen is one of the best blood purifiers and most effective nerve tonics. If the poisonous waste matter called carbon monoxide (which should be expelled from the lungs by exhalations) is retained, then the blood becomes impure, harming not only the lungs but the stomach, liver, and brain also. Forest bathing provides an effective way of connecting with nature and improving our ability to breathe and expand our life force energy.

The Indigenous and ancient populations have been connecting with nature for more than 50,000 years. The most important thing is to associate being in nature with feeling good, and recharging and recalibrating your aura (the energy field surrounding the body). If you simply go outside and center yourself in nature, whether it's a forest or not, then you're 'forest bathing.'

Try it for yourself with these 10 easy steps:

Before beginning, store your electronic device away until the end of this exercise.

1. The first step is to locate a local forest. If that's not possible, you can also use any patch of nature with trees, lakes, ponds, or an open grassy field.

2. Once a location is identified and you are there, stand still and recognize your body being in that space. Begin to use your sense of sight by walking a path or trail to

notice the details surrounding you in this environment. Observe the landscape and notice what draws your attention the most such as the trees, bushes, plants, flowers, etc.

3. Once an object has caught your attention, slowly approach it to view it at a closer distance.

4. Experience touching the bark up close, feeling the texture (e.g. Birch trees have a very smooth touch) to activate your senses.

5. Notice any sounds in the air from leaves. These noises may also be birds chirping, or even water splashing from a lake or river.

6. Take a few slow deep breaths through your nose and exhale out your mouth. With your eyes closed, notice the smells of nature. Do not breathe too loudly, but rather attempt to have your noises blend in with the natural sounds of nature. Closing your eyes during this part gives you access to mindful engagement with your other senses such as smell. Certain tree scents have particular benefits. Cedar and birch trees - among other plant life - produce phytoncides which increase the number of disease-fighting white blood cells in the body.

7. Try taking a leaf off a tree and crushing it with your hands, releasing the smell. Imagine what medicinal properties that leaf may have.

8. At some point during your walking path, find a log or dry area of grass to sit on. Take the time to turn your focus more inward.

9. Repeat steps 2 through 7 as many times as you need.

10. Traditionally, most forest bathing walks are commenced with a drink of herbal tea. If tea doesn't hold a calming effect for you, drink a cup of water during this reflective process. While drinking tea or water, take your time to prepare to re-engage back into society, but keep your awareness as you do.

If you're struggling to find time for this exercise, then here is another way of experiencing forest bathing without having to go outside. Whether you're at home or the office, oxygen-producing houseplants can boost your mental strength, immunity, and energy levels.

Indoor plants to add to your home or office:

1. Pathos

2. Peace Lily

3. Areca Palm

4. Snake Plant

5. Weeping Fig

6. Orchid

7. Spider Plant

8. Christmas Cactus

9. Dumb Cane

10. Chrysanthemum

So, whether you just need to breathe and unwind from a long day, or if you ever find yourself feeling a bit of depression, anxiety, or stress, try implementing this exercise to remind you to unplug and reconnect with nature. Receive beneficial health properties and watch it lead to transformational gains in your life.

Healing from Trauma: Daily Practices for Rebuilding Self-Love
By Rachel Lynn Gladstone

This chapter shows you two simple practices for overcoming trauma and turning stress and anxiety into peace and self-love. Done daily, both mirror work and box/square breathing will totally transform you and your life.

Great for:

- Rebuilding self-love and self-confidence after a traumatic event or period.

- Reducing stress and/or anxiety levels and improving the quality of sleep.

- Developing a daily practice to improve concentration and focus.

After surviving years of mental and physical abuse, three years ago, I finally found the strength and courage to leave my abusive and toxic relationship. It was not easy after suffering from severe anxiety and depression and two attempts at killing myself. I finally came to the realization that my life did mean something.

As a survivor of domestic violence, I can empathize with whatever big life challenges you're currently going through. I share my struggles and victories with you so that you can see the potential you have for overcoming your trauma and rebuilding your self-esteem. I always encourage seeking out professional care when you feel like you need a little extra help as this is not medical advice.

If you're willing to put in the work and undertake a regular practice of self-healing, you'll transform your entire life. Ask yourself, "What is my freedom, happiness, self-esteem, and life worth to me?"

I practice the following two exercises daily, and they've been a massive part of my recovery and success. These exercises helped me overcome my fear and self-doubt as I rebuilt my life. By applying these techniques daily, you will regain the natural self-esteem and self-confidence you simply put aside in the face of your traumatic or challenging life situation. It was never lost, it was just protecting you by hiding away. Regular practice of these exercises will enable you to reclaim safety so the real you can re-emerge.

Practice 1: Mirror Work

Mirror work was an enormous part of my recovery, and still plays a huge part in my life. When I started practicing mirror work, I had low to zero self-esteem left. I no longer believed in myself. But no matter how difficult it was, I would force myself out of bed, stand in front of the mirror and remind myself of my worth. I've made it part of my daily routine and I am living proof that this exercise truly does transform.

Mirror work is designed to aid in self-development, shifting the way you see yourself, and grounding you in your body. Other potential benefits of mirror work are an increased sense of self-confidence, inner peace, and a deeper sense of trust in yourself and your life. Louise Hay in *Mirror Work: 21 Days to Heal Your Life* says looking in the mirror is important "because the mirror reflects back to you the feelings you have about yourself. It makes you immediately aware of where you are resisting and where you are open and flowing.

It clearly shows you what thoughts you will need to change if you want to have a joyous, fulfilling life."

Step 1: Write down your affirmations

Affirmations are positive statements that can help you to challenge and overcome self-sabotaging and negative thoughts. When you repeat them often and believe in them, you can start to make positive changes. For example, evidence suggests that affirmations can help you to perform better at work.

Some examples of positive affirmations are:

- I am confident.

- I am happy driving my new car.

- I enjoy my home.

- I believe in my dreams.

- I am doing my best every day.

- I love myself for who I am.

- I am in charge of my own happiness.

- I accept 100% responsibility for my own life.

- The best is yet to come.

- I am grateful for every day.

- I love my life.

- I enjoy getting up early.

- I am worthy of a healthy, loving relationship.

- I am beautiful.

- I am strong.

- I take pride in my work.

Tip for coaches:

I first like to tell my client to sit in a quiet area of their home and write down five affirmations promoting self-love. Know that this can be difficult for your client because most of them have a hard time finding anything positive to say about themselves and their lives. So make them aware that no matter how difficult this may be, they need to look deep inside themselves and if they can't think of five affirmations, have them start with three. Most clients just need you to list some examples of affirmations and then they usually find affirmations that relate to them. They can always add to this list later, just make sure they know to truly believe in what they write down.

Step 2: Stand in front of the mirror

After writing down your five affirmations, stand in front of the mirror and repeat the list three times with confidence while looking at yourself. This may trigger emotions that you've never felt and may even make you cry. But that's okay, your subconscious is loving all that positivity. It's incredibly healing!!

Do this daily for 30 days. Can you totally transform your life in just 30 days? Well, maybe not totally, but you can plant the seeds needed to transform your life. As you continue to do your mirror work daily, these seeds you've planted will develop into new, healthy habits of mind that open the door to a joyous and fulfilling life. The more compliments you feed your subconscious mind, the more loving your relationship with yourself will be. This is a technique I apply in my daily life and I also encourage all you coaches out there to practice it.

Practice 2: Square/Box Breathing

This next exercise is something I personally can't live without. For years I struggled with anxiety and panic attacks. Even though I logically understood that I was manifesting my symptoms (fight or flight behavior), and even though I knew that my body could not feel two conflicting emotions at once, I still allowed fear to take over. I knew my mind was in control and that I could stop the anxiety at any moment but I chose to give it power over me.

But then I discovered proper breathing techniques and it was a game-changer. I promise you, when you focus on your breathing your mind can't focus on anything else. It's the most satisfying feeling to know that you can regain control of your life and take back your power by simply taking five minutes out of your day to breathe.

Square breathing is also known as box breathing. It is a technique used in a variety of settings, from doctors' and therapists' offices to yoga studios and meditation centers. Even Navy SEALs use box breathing to stay calm and improve their concentration in extremely tense tactical situations.

The benefits of box breathing:

- Helps you cope with panic and stress when feeling overwhelmed.

- Aids sleep when you are experiencing insomnia.

- Helps you refocus when you are having a busy or stressful day.

- Eases panic, anxiety, stress, and worry.

Get ready

Go to a comfortable room in your home, preferably a quiet place. Sit down in a chair in an upright position, with your hands laid flat out on your legs.

We are going to apply the following breathing method. As the name suggests, the pattern of breathing can be symbolized by a box or square. Each repetition or circuit of the practice has four parts (like a box). Imagine a box or focus on something in this room in front of you in a square shape, such as a picture frame.

Step 1: Inhale through the nose to a count of four, so the lungs are completely full of air.

Step 2: Hold the air in your lungs for a count of four.

Step 3: Exhale through the mouth to a count of four, so all of the air is out of the lungs.

Step 4: Hold the lungs in an empty state for a count of four.

Step 5: Repeat steps 1 through 4 for a total of at least 5 minutes. If comfortable, you can increase to a count of 8.

Once you have this breathing technique down, it's helpful to use in bed before going to sleep, to help you relax.

These exercises both work best when you are in a relaxed state of mind. Email me at embracenlp@gmail.com for my relaxation hypnosis audio to help you get the most out of your personal development.

PART 3
MAGICAL MANIFESTING:

TECHNIQUES TO ATTRACT YOUR DREAMS

Your Future Life Now: Accelerating Your Dreams by Changing Your Identity

By Justin Wenck, Ph.D.

Your current life is a reflection of who you currently are. To have a life with a different level of abundance, relationships, or health, you'll have to change at the identity level and become the person who already lives in that abundant environment. This exercise creates an easy-to-use structure and practice for becoming that person at the subconscious level in as little as five minutes a day.

Great for:

• Those dissatisfied in one or more areas of their life and dream for more.

• Those who hustle and take action but yet still haven't achieved what they want.

• Those who believe that achieving their dreams can feel easy and natural.

• Achieving results in as little as five minutes per day.

Have you ever wanted to make one of your dreams come true, but every time you tried to take a step towards it, no matter how much effort, training, or study, you ended up right back where you started? Perhaps it's the career you've always wanted, a better relationship, or just getting your health on point. Maybe you manage to make minor improvements, but it feels like it is taking forever, or still out of reach despite your best efforts. You're intelligent and hard-working. Otherwise, you wouldn't be reading a book of exercises to improve your life. Naturally, you wonder, what should you do?

That's where the "Your Future Life Now" tool I've developed comes in. I use this tool to help people transform quickly and easily. It uses Identity Installation Questions (IIQs) that change you from the person who is *wanting* the dream to *being* the person who already *has* the thing you want. IIQs presuppose that you already are the person who has the life that you want. For example, if you want to improve your fitness, you may ask yourself, "Why is it so enjoyable for me to have a world-class body?" I'll share more about IIQs in a bit, but first, let's look at why it is important to change our identity.

I'm sure you know people who have components of the life you want to have. You might know one person who is more athletic, another who is more attractive, another with more digits in the bank account, and yet another with the love and friends you've always wanted. Often people will dismiss what these people have by thinking they are "lucky" or have "good genes," but when you're honest, you know they have what you admire because they live differently than how you do. They have a different identity in that particular area of life than you have.

When Arnold Swarnzenggar was at the top of his body-building game, how do you think he felt about going to the gym for hours at a time? (Hint: In "Pumping Iron" he describes working out as being more physically enjoyable than just about any other activity.) Concerning the gym, Arnold's identity was that of someone who enjoyed building a world-class body worthy of championships. That identity is what enabled him to spend all those hours in the gym and eat the right foods, which resulted in the physical results of a champion.

Most people have it backwards and want to take massive actions until their eyeballs bleed and grind it out till their dreams happen (or rather, don't happen). Then they experience burnout and feel as if they've failed themselves. For most of us, that just isn't sustainable. The key is to go to a much deeper level where our behaviors come from: our identity. For example, who are you in the area of relationships? Money? Fun? Health?

I remember the first personal development seminar I attended eight years ago in Scottsdale, Arizona. I went because I was sick of being in relationships that went nowhere. I felt I wasn't getting any younger and was scared of dying alone, or worse: dying with someone who made me miserable. At one point, the coach put us into a highly receptive state and I was asked to fill in the blank: "I am ____ of Relationships" and my immediate response was "scared". Wow, no wonder all my relationships until then had gone nowhere. Who wants something "scary" in their life? No one!

I started asking myself, "Why am I always surrounded by love and amazing people whom I'm deeply connected to? Why is it so easy and fun to be in relationships?" Eventually, I became someone who "enjoys relationships" because I was able to strengthen and enjoy the connections I already had, which made it easier to find new connections that led to even stronger and more fulfilling relationships.

Once you know what you want, the "Your Future Life Now" exercise empowers you to have the identity that will make getting what you want easy. If you are "fun, easy, and loving" in relationships, how much more excited are you to pursue and maintain friendships and a romantic partnership? Even if it's just 5% easier, it pays off with huge dividends over your lifetime.

This exercise uses one of the most powerful words in the English language to accomplish the shifting of your identity. What is this magical word? The word is "why".

Like any powerful tool, such as a scalpel, the word "why" can cut as much as it can heal. The mind is an incredible solution generation machine and anytime you present it with a challenge it can't help but generate solutions. This is why the Tony Robbins quote, "The quality of your life is determined by the quality of your questions," rings so true.

If you ask yourself, "Why am I so angry all the time?" the mind will further reinforce your state of anger by providing a laundry list of supporting information: people around you are incompetent, you're not getting what you need, your father was an angry man so how could you be different, anger is the only thing that gets things done, etc. The end result is simply more anger.

What happens when we flip this around and ask ourselves a question that presupposes that a noble attribute we would like to embody is already true? E.g. "Why does money pile up in my life?" When we ask these types of questions, our mind starts to find reasons why it's true. Consciously, you might not be able to come up with any reasons why it's true, but your subconscious will be working in the background to find the answer. After repeated daily practice, the reasons will become conscious and the identity that was once aspirational will become true in your mind, and reflected by your behaviors. Naturally, your external environment follows suit.

Since the questions in the practice effectively install a new identity in you, that's why I call them Identity Installation Questions (IIQs).

My own story is a great example of how this exercise creates dramatic results in an accelerated way. In January 2020, I was deeply unhappy in my technical career and wanting to figure out a way to take a year off. I envisioned myself being in amazing shape, with long flowing hair instead of my usually conservative cut, in a tropical area teaching many eager students. In my vision, I felt abundant and knew that money was piling up in my life. Students and mentors were thanking and congratulating me on all I'd done.

My logical plan was to save up money from each paycheck and my calculations said I'd be able to take time away starting in July 2021 and then I'd focus on my appearance and teaching. I began practicing and perfecting my "Your Future Life Now" tool starting in February of 2020 and a few months later I was able to refinance my home and take cash out, which put me above the dollar amount I set to be able to take a year off. Being stubborn, I still held off on taking my time off. Then through a series of events and connections, I found out how to take a paid leave from my job starting in November 2020. That's nine months sooner than my logical, action-oriented planning would have allowed.

In July 2021 I had my most downloaded and listened to podcast ever, thus bringing to my fruition my desire to teach a large audience. As for being tropical, I'm editing this chapter in Roatan, Honduras during a scuba trip. Oh, and I have the long hair I was dreaming about too. So my 2-3 year vision came true in half the time thanks to this exercise. I've had countless people I've taught this exercise to who have already felt like they are on the way towards making their dream a reality, and I know it will work for you.

Steps:

1. Envision your ideal future life 2-3 years from now (1-2 min). Focus on the full expression of your dreams. If you want more money or a better relationship, what else does that give you? What do you see? What are you or others talking about? How do you feel?

2. Ask Identity Installation Questions (IIQs) to become the person who has the life you want (2-3 min). The questions presuppose that you already are the person who has the life that you want. Mentally ask yourself the question and rest in the experience that follows for 1 or 2 seconds. A conscious answer is not required. You might experience a feeling, a thought, or nothing at all. Whatever you experience, let it go after a few moments and go to the next question until you get through all of them.

Here are IIQs that support most desires:

1. Why am I always surrounded by bliss and happiness no matter what?

2. Why am I able to do so much in so little time?

3. Why am I always surrounded by love and amazing people to whom I'm deeply connected?

4. Why am I so brilliant, so genius, and so able to tap into Source for instant inspiration?

5. Why am I so good at making, keeping, and multiplying money?

6. Why does the Universe always have my back?

7. Why do my dreams and goals come to me with such ease and speed?

8. Why am I so good at taking care of my health?

9. Why do I have such a clear vision of what I want for my life?

10. Why do I become healthier and more attractive as I age?

11. Why am I surrounded by so much beauty?

12. Why is my life filled with so much fun and adventure?

13. Why is it so easy to turn any situation into an opportunity for joy, love, or growth?

14. Why am I always surrounded by love?

15. Why does money pile up in my life?

16. Why is it so easy to realize I am healed?

17. Why do I love myself so much?

18. Ensure you've asked key IIQs to support your future life (30 sec). You can re-ask yourself any of the IIQs or ask your own IIQ to support the future life you wish to create now. For example, if your current focus is releasing body fat, you might ask yourself, "Why is it so easy for me to release body fat and feel safe and comfortable with the new attention I receive?"

19. Repeat this exercise once or twice daily to bring your future life into existence now. Although you're looking 2 to 3 years in the future, be prepared for your dreams to begin coming into your life much sooner in unsuspecting ways. Let go of the "How" or the "When" and focus on the "What."

For a guided audio version of this exercise please visit:
www.justinwenck.com/AYLV3

Tips for using it with a client:

Although the suggested IIQ's will install an identity with clarity of purpose, most people struggle with deciding what they want to achieve in the next 2 to 3 years. The most common answer is, "I don't know." By asking, "What if you did know?" you will get an answer, but it will often be a surface answer, such as "More money." This is where a coach can help dig deeper to get to a desire that brings true meaning into the client's life. Through a series of questions, a coach can help the client go from the 'means' goal of "more money" to an 'ends' goal of "enough financial abundance so that I can take my family on the travel adventures I desire at least 4 weeks a year." This can then be made more vivid by flushing out the visuals, the sounds, and the feelings that complete this vision of their future life.

Looking at how you'd like your life to be in the next 2-3 years is a very powerful part of this exercise. Why not 1 year? Why not next week? With shorter time periods we tend to limit what we can accomplish with linear thinking. I made X this year, I can probably only make X + 5% if I'm lucky next year. In 2-3 years literally anything can happen. Even with a corporate job, it's possible that a merger or acquisition could result in a 20% raise. I know because this is happening to me right now. The only difference is that with this exercise we're going to design that dramatic difference instead of being a passive receiver. As Robert Noyce says, "Don't be encumbered by history. Go off and do something wonderful."

The Elemental Transformation Method: Transform Unproductive Energies to Bring About Positive Change
By Tami Zenoble

In this exercise, you will be working with the elements of nature (earth, air, fire, and water) to release unwanted patterns and replace them with new, more productive ones. It's great for shifting limiting beliefs and stuck emotions or letting go of a challenging life situation, so you can move forward and create the life you want.

Great for:

• Shifting limiting beliefs that are holding you back from your best life.

• Reconnecting with nature and learning how to use elemental energies to cleanse emotions and stoke your internal fire.

• Those who are emotionally stuck and need a way to release and reset.

• Learning a method for moving out of situations or patterns that no longer positively serve you.

When my marriage of 13 years came to an end, I was devastated. The pain that I felt at times was unbearable. It was as if someone close to me had died. I found myself drawn to nature, specifically a river near where I live. I would hike down to the river and spend hours exploring and wading in the cold water.

One day, I was sitting on the shore in the sun, when a wave of emotion gripped my chest and tears were streaming down my face. Looking for something to comfort me, I picked up a smooth stone that was lying near me. Instinctively, I held it to my solar plexus and began to imagine that I was releasing the uncomfortable energy I was feeling into the stone.

I began to go over everything in my mind that had transpired over the last six months and one by one, released them into the stone with long deep breaths. After a while, I ran out of things to put into the stone. I then threw the stone out into the rushing river as far as I possibly could. I was amazed at how much lighter I felt. The painful emotions were gone and I felt like I could start creating a new life for myself.

I began to call this exercise 'A Stones' Throw'. I was always only a stones' throw away from releasing what was burdening me so I could take a fresh look at any challenging situation I was facing and see a path for how to move forward. I was having such great success with this exercise, I started sharing it with other people.

Susan was an ER nurse who had been living on a 51-foot yacht for five years and decided it was time for a change. She left her job and purchased a house in another state, planning on selling the yacht after she got settled. Every month she had to make sure the yacht was being maintained, stay in constant contact with the person who was helping her sell it, and make the slip rental and insurance payments. At one point, due to gasket failure on one of the engines, the yacht almost sank and the boat had to be taken out of the water to do the repairs.

After all of this and 18 months of people looking but not buying, Susan began to experience extreme anxiety over the situation. She tried donating the yacht to get a tax write-off. She tried selling it dirt cheap. The more she struggled and tried to make something happen, the more difficult the situation became.

One day we were out walking on a nature trail by a beautiful rushing river talking about the boat situation that seemed to be consuming her life. I suggested she try A Stone's Throw. She looked around but didn't see a stone to pick up. At my feet was a stone partly buried in the dirt on the trail. I said, "Why don't you use this one?" and she replied, "I can't use that. It's the tip of a huge boulder that's under the ground!" I said, "No it's not." I gave it a couple of good kicks with my hiking boot, dislodged it, handed it to her, and said, "It's just a boat."

We walked down to the river and I guided her through the process until she was ready to release the stone. She threw it as hard as she could out into the river, and with a big sigh, she looked at me and said, "Wow! I feel so much better!" I saw a big shift in Susan's perception after that. She reassessed the situation and decided that it wasn't worth the stress or the cost to continue trying to sell the yacht, so she decided to give it away.

She found the perfect person and signed it over to him and never looked back. She never doubted that she had made the right decision. The process enabled Susan to experience a profound sense of being able to let go of the burden, no matter the cost.

Since then, I have developed a method that incorporates A Stones Throw, but more fully addresses what is occurring on an energetic level and paves the way for positive change.

It incorporates a shamanic drum beat to entrain the brain into a theta state, which will allow you to release what no longer serves you and replace it with something that will lead you in a more positive direction. Listening to this drum beat, your brain will be exhibiting the same wave patterns it would if you were in a deep meditative state, yet you will be fully awake.

When you're letting go of something, it's useful to have something positive in mind you want to replace it with. If you don't know what you want to replace it with, simply set the intention that you will remain open to a positive change in your life. This will give you a different perspective and reprogram the subconscious mind to be more receptive to positive change.

Steps to experiencing the Elemental Transformation Method:

To fully experience this method, it is best to be in a place in nature, near a body of water. If you choose to do this in a river or stream, you want to find a place where you can safely enter the water without the danger of being swept away. A shallow, gently flowing place near the shore is suitable. If you like, you can find a place where you can wade in further. Once again, pay attention to the flow of the river. This exercise can also be done in a lake where you can go in farther without worrying about the current. At the ocean, you can simply stand at the edge and let the waves rush in around your ankles.

1. Before entering the water, find a comfortable spot to sit and listen to a simple repetitive drum beat that cycles 4 to 6 beats per second for 5 to 10 minutes. If you like, you can use a drum or rattle yourself using a four-count.

If you prefer, you can listen to a recording of a shamanic drum beat on your phone using earbuds.

2. Do A Stones' Throw. Pick a stone and focus on what you want to release. Thought by thought, blow what you are releasing into the stone. Continue this process until you feel satisfied. Don't rush yourself. Allow for plenty of time. When you are ready, throw the stone into the water.

3. Next, you want to enter the water and make yourself comfortable. If you are in a river, you can prop yourself against a rock or hold onto a log. Bring your awareness into the bottoms of your feet and your seat if you are sitting. Feel the earth supporting you. Take a deep breath and release it deep into the earth. Take time to reflect on all the ways the Earth supports us. She provides abundant food, shelter, fuel, and water.

4. Next, feel the sun on your skin. Taking a breath in, imagine the sun's rays entering through the top of your head and flowing down your central channel, all the way down your legs and into the earth. With your next breath, bring the sun's rays in through the top of your head, but this time, expand your rib cage with your breath allowing them to feed your own central sun. Feel the warmth in your solar plexus as your inner fire expands. Feel it expand past the confines of your body, let it get as big as you are comfortable with. As you stoke this fire, imagine it burning up what no longer serves you into ash. From the ashes, rises your will to move forward into a more positive flow.

5. Finally, focus on the flow of the water around you. Water holds information and the ancient wisdom of the ancestors. Allow the water to cleanse your emotions.

Absorb whatever information and messages the water holds for you. Spend some time quietly listening. When we heal the waters within, we heal the waters without. When you are ready, slowly open your eyes.

You have now worked with earth, air, fire, and water on an elemental level. You may want to record your experience in a journal so you may reference it. Sometimes we receive information that doesn't make sense at that moment but will later. Also, you may want to record your dreams, as they may contain information that will assist you in this process.

Tips for coaches to use this exercise:

This exercise works well with small groups. If you like, you can drum for them and coach them through the exercise almost like a guided meditation. I like to do the exercise alongside my students. It helps you to connect to the experience and lead them through it in a relaxed manner. Really feel into it and don't rush through any of the steps. Remember, you are reprogramming the subconscious mind so you want to use positive reinforcement. Instead of speaking about anything negative that is being released, speak about the positive energy that is replacing it. This way the final impression in their mind is a positive one.

To assist you on your journey, download a very special, 10-minute Shamanic drumming and rattling track, recorded live at Breitenbush Hot Springs, when you subscribe to my email list: www.PhoenixMoonRetreats.com.

The Unified Field Manifestation
By Derek Loudermilk

The Unified Field Manifestation is a group manifestation exercise. You will use this to create a specific future reality (life or business outcome) for one of the group members. This is a powerful supplement to any personal manifestation or creative practice.

Great for:

- Quickly manifesting a big result in life or business.

- Experiencing the power of group and collective consciousness.

- Those who like evidence-based magical practices.

"That was the most powerful experience I've had in my life!" – participant of a Unified Field Manifestation

Doing the Unified Field Manifestation will make you feel more connected to life than you have ever felt, in alignment with your highest calling, powerful beyond belief, and of great service. I have seen ideal life situations manifest for people, sometimes in a matter of days or weeks, after doing this exercise.

Most manifestation techniques focus on what you as an individual can do with your own level of consciousness. The Unified Field Manifestation (UFM) takes manifesting to an entirely new level to harness the power of the human collective. The UFM is a manifestation technique that is done with a small group of people (8 is ideal, can be a group of 5-15) and will allow you to manifest specific results for a member of the group. Ideally, you focus your efforts on a single receiver per session, and you can schedule sessions for the other members at different times.

When I discovered Lynne McTaggart's healing process called 'Power of 8' (https://youtu.be/HTORJd3s3Ws), I knew right away I could merge this with many of the manifestation techniques I knew to create a brand new type of manifestation process for groups and entrepreneurship masterminds.

Lynne's research, which has over 20 years of experimental data showing effective group healing, highlights just how powerful our shared intentions can be. I was particularly excited about the 'rebound effect' that McTaggart observed - people sending the intention experienced just as much healing as the receivers. This is also called the universal law of reciprocity or Ayni to the Mayans – *what you give, you will receive.* I knew that if we could also harness this reciprocity effect for the benefit of the entire group, all my clients would experience tremendous success.

We did this exercise every month as an experiment in the League of Superconductors - the Quantum Business Mastermind I run. We ended the year with a 100% success rate for manifesting the business-related outcome that the receiver intended. We manifested successful biz launches, romantic partners, TV appearances, filled retreats, and more.

Not only that, but I was blown away by the immense sense of connection and power that was generated during each UFM session; we also had a 100% success rate in making me so emotional I cried.

Why UFM works (for you left-brained thinkers):

- When you set intentions for others, a quantum tunnel is created between you and the other person that amplifies both your and their personal power.

- Your intention is sent in the form of bio-photons (biologically created light particles that transmit information) - time and distance do not matter.

- When people share and send the same intention, their individual identity signatures merge and they connect to the unified field (electromagnetic field/universal consciousness), which amplifies the effect.

- You regenerate your own bio-photons through the process, which is likely why we experience the rebound mirror effect and also get the benefit when we send energy to another person.

- Nobody wants to waste their chance to manifest a result with a frivolous intention, so people only ask for others to intend a result for them that is truly important.

- There is power in the asking - when you ask others to support your intention, you have already begun to create that future reality.

It can be done in person, or remotely on a video call. The whole process of discussing and clarifying intentions, doing the UFM process, and debriefing usually takes about an hour. I recommend focusing on only one receiver each session to keep the intention as clean and clear as possible.

Unified Field Manifestation Steps:

1. Prepare your intentions

For each Unified Field Manifestation session, every group member prepares their own intention that they would like to manifest, using the following steps:

1. Describe the outcome you want the group to intend for you, using all 5 senses.

2. Come up with an intention statement and "intention movie scene" that all the other members can use as a starting point to understand what you want to manifest.

3. Use the questions Who, What, When, Where, Why, and How.

4. Describe the feelings you are experiencing once your goal has arrived.

Choosing an appropriate intention:

- In our mastermind, we usually had a few people bring an idea of something they wanted to manifest. Each person would share, and we would vote on which intention we were most excited to put our efforts towards.

- Choose an intention that has a strong emotional charge for the receiver and senders. What are the feelings you expect to feel when this intention comes true?

- Ask clarifying questions about what it would look and feel like when the intention comes true. What is the exact moment when you will know the intention has come true? What will it feel like?

- Make sure that everyone is on the same page for the intention. Frame the intention in a phrase: "Our intention is that..."

When you share your intention with the group, make a vow to them that you will do everything in your power to make this intention a reality.

2. Warming up

Prior to each session, encourage each member to get into a positive, calm, and powerful state by meditating for 15 minutes (using a theta wave binaural beat) and then doing a Power Pose for 2 minutes (taking up as much space as you can with your arms and legs spread - like a starfish or big gorilla. This reduces cortisol and boosts testosterone, which allows your body to become a solid base for your intention).

Then you can do a group warm-up at the beginning of each session or call, using one or more of the following techniques:

- Diaphragm breathing. Three deep breaths with audible sighs to reset the nervous system.

- Getting into our bodies using our senses. Close your eyes and feel your toes in your shoes. Listen to the environment around you.

- Focus your attention on your heart and send light and love from your heart to the rest of your body.

- 2 minutes of Loving Kindness (metta) meditation: Think of all of those that you love, then friends, acquaintances, and finally enemies, send them the thought: "May they be well and free from suffering."

3. Sending the Intention

Any member of the group can lead the visualization. In our mastermind, each member took turns guiding the group into the process - they made up the details on the spot with no previous experience. It is helpful to ask the senders to form a mental vision of holding hands in a circle, standing around a fire, standing in a clearing in the woods, or another such scene that creates unity of the group. We always play Choku Rei audio (https://youtu.be/LdFpw0XuHDc) but feel free to use any audio that sets the right mood for you.

The job of the receiver is to open his/her heart to receive. The senders will send the intention down through their hearts.

Cycle the intention through your focused thoughts for the full 10 minutes and send it to the receiver. ou can shorten or extend the length of time as desired.

After sending the intention

We usually budget 10-20 minutes after the process to debrief. People love to share their experience of what was happening during the process - because it is so powerful. We have found that most of the senders become aware of additional insights that help the receiver in their manifestation process - imagery and symbols, ways of being, and actual precognition of events are all experienced and can be relayed to the receiver.

Example intention:

Sasha wants to run her first successful retreat and asks the group to intend this to happen.

We ask questions like: What do you want the retreat to feel like? Is there a specific moment when you will know it was a success? What will the ideal retreat setting look like? How many people do you want to attend? Why is this important to you?

Then we craft a specific statement of intent like: "We intend for Sasha to be successful with her first retreat. There will be 10 women in attendance in the jungle of Costa Rica, all the right people will show up. At the closing ceremony, everyone is sharing from their heart about the dramatic progress they have made during the retreat. Sasha feels at ease and powerful because she is finally doing the work she is meant to do in the world."

When we drop into the intention process, often, specific names, faces, locations, prices, numbers, clothing, events, will present themselves in the mind's eye of multiple members of the group - these can often give momentum to the process.

Keep track of your progress for your intention and report back to the group. Often the receiver will experience an immediate benefit within 24 hours - a new client signs up, an unexpected invitation, or a brainstorm for an idea.

There is a skill in sending your intention - in research, psi effects, like intention sending, have been shown to work best with a relaxed focus and an awareness outside of one's self (dissolution of the ego). Here are a couple of ways to practice projecting your intention and awareness:

- Sending loving intentions to your plants.

- Send an image from your mind into a jar of water - then write that image on a piece of paper and rubber band it around the jar (not showing the image). Have the other group members intuit the image that is in the water

- Bless your food and water with a specific intention.

Case Study: Daniel Brisbon

"When people have been through the Unified Field Manifestation, they seem to step into action effortlessly and without hesitation." - Daniel Brisbon

Daniel Brisbon is a Nature Connected coach (and the author of the exercise in this book "Radical Daydreaming") and was a member of League of Superconductors for a year when we did this exercise monthly. He has since started using it with his students at the Nature Connected Coaching Institute. Daniel says that one of the benefits of this process is it encourages him to spend a lot of time discussing what it is his students want to create in the world but haven't yet, and their relationship to their vision.

One time, Daniel did this exercise and it was so powerful that people were unable to speak for 15 minutes afterwards and had their state changed for the rest of the day. Daniel often did the exercise for a bit longer - 15-20 minutes. He tells his students, it is important to think of this not as a New Age technique, but as something that has been effective for humans for millennia and passed down from generation to generation. Many of his students said that they had never been so present before for an activity or for themselves in their life. Daniel instructs his students to imagine giving the intention as a gift to the receiver.

Daniel says that for practitioners of this exercise the skill comes in knowing how quickly or slowly the group should be led into the exercise. If it is a group that is already close or in a peaceful state, you may be able to start more quickly, but sometimes you may take half an hour of visualizing to get to the right state to send the intention. "If you are in-person, it is easier to read their body language to know how quickly to drop in", said Daniel.

Radical Daydreaming: Visualize Your Desired Future Through Your Empowered Past
By Daniel Brisbon

Radical Daydreaming is a visualization practice that trains you to break through your own mental and emotional barriers so that you can access your higher intelligence. It is a creative, fun, and effective mental practice to train your mind to focus on empowering memories and experiencing expansive love-based feelings in your body, in order to successfully imagine the ideal future that you *choose to create* in your daily life.

Great for:

- Learning how to bypass your fight/flight/freeze state in high-intensity situations and become a high performer.

- Accessing your higher intelligence and thriving in the face of challenges and stressful future events.

- Overcoming the habit of living on 'auto-pilot' and instead becoming a conscious creator.

- Empowering your imagination to find potential outcomes and opportunities on your way to completing "impossible" projects

---

Visualization is the art of focusing your mind to consciously imagine a future event in your life as if it was happening in this present moment. It is the mindful creation of a mental image of an event in your life that has not happened yet. Visualization is consciously choosing the mental movie that is playing on the movie screen of your mind. You do it all the time whether or not you are consciously aware of it.

Radical Daydreaming is my unique twist on visualization that I taught myself in my career as a downhill mountain bike racer. In racing, I had to learn to overcome my mind and emotions to successfully ride gracefully down rock gardens and over massive jumps. When I had to ride a challenging feature for the first time, it was difficult to imagine riding smoothly without immediately visualizing myself crashing and getting badly hurt.

I learned very quickly in my years of mountain bike racing that if I felt contracted feelings in my body and thought negative thoughts in my mind, I would fulfill that prophecy and most likely crash my bike. But if I felt loose and relaxed in my body and thought empowering thoughts in my mind, then I noticed I was racing smoothly and putting up results that I never expected or imagined possible. This visualization practice was literally one of the greatest building blocks in my journey of becoming a professional cyclist.

I taught myself to visualize an empowering past experience, or anchor memory, that inspired me. Then I was able to tune up my mind and body to be in the calm and relaxed state that I needed them in to ride my bike like a graceful bat out of hell. During my years of racing, I learned that my internal state (thinking and feeling) had the greatest impact and influence on my external performance. I knew that I had to feel successful before I could ride successfully.

And this is what I am going to teach you. This exercise will show you how to channel and visualize your empowered past in order to visualize your ideal future. You will be remembering a past positive event and bringing that feeling into your future.

Steps To Practice Radical Daydreaming:

Sit or lie down somewhere quiet and close your eyes. Your Radical Daydreaming practice is about to begin. Read through these steps before doing your visualization practice or listen to my guided meditation (link in Bio).

1. Choose an upcoming future event that you would like to visualize in this present moment. It could be your day today, an upcoming challenging event, or your ideal life 3 years from now.

   Close your eyes and choose an area of your life that might be creating tension, anxiety, or any contracting feeling/thinking inside of yourself.

2. Choose the feeling you need to embody to create your ideal outcome for your future event. Choose one or two feelings or emotions (joy, peace, inspiration, love, power, freedom, happiness, confidence).

   If you are having trouble choosing your ideal love-based state, then I highly recommend using gratitude. Gratitude is one of the most powerful and transformative tools that we can focus on and it unifies you with the reality you are seeking.

3. Now take a few more deep anchoring breaths. Close your eyes and allow your mind to navigate through the ocean of your past memories to find a memory where you strongly felt and embodied that desired feeling. This is your anchor memory. The more vivid it is the better.

4. Continue taking several deep breaths. Do a body scan from head to toe, becoming aware of and releasing any tension in the muscles and joints that you might be

holding. Relax the body and nervous system. Replay your anchor memory and imagine it is happening right now. Bring in all of your senses (sight, sound, smell, touch, taste).

5. Once you feel your anchor memory completely in the present moment then shift your focus to this upcoming future event. Visualize and imagine yourself embodying the feeling from your past memory as you play the movie of this upcoming challenge. See yourself in the flow, engaging with the world the way that you want to engage.

   Who is the future self that you are choosing to become?

   What do you see yourself doing or creating that you weren't aware of before?

   What does your intuition tell you about possible action steps to take to make this visualization into a reality?

6. And whatever you are visualizing be sure to believe! Go back and forth between visualizing your anchor memory and your upcoming event until you are visualizing your future with creativity and belief. Why is this possible for you? Who are you doing this for?

7. After you are done visualizing, start writing down whatever new thoughts or insights came to you from this exercise. What did you notice? What is that telling you? What is that teaching you?

This may take time and focus before your mind starts to associate the love-based state that you choose with the trigger/situation that you are visualizing. But over time it will happen! Just keep focusing on what you choose to be doing and what you choose to be feeling.

You have power over the thoughts you choose to focus on in the mind. So choose empowering and expansive thoughts. Focus on moments in your life where you felt love, connection, confidence, or gratitude. And then in that state bring your mind back to the future event you are visualizing.

Visualize every little detail of this future event. The more detailed you make it in your mind then the more real it feels. Use all of your senses.

This is a practice. It will require time, consistency, and intensity and I know if you stay consistent with it, you will start to experience unimaginable results.

Tips For Using This Practice With A Client:

Radical Daydreaming requires:

- A future challenging event

- An anchor memory (the more specific the better)

- An expansive emotion (like love or gratitude)

- Imagination

- Belief

As a coach, make sure your client has named all of these before the visualization exercise. Except for belief, because belief is created and empowered through this practice.

- You can guide your client through this visualization practice or you can invite them to do the practice on their own. For a client's first time doing this, I recommend guiding them through the visualization practice.

- This visualization practice can range from 5 to 30 minutes. Or longer if you'd like!

- Your brain is only capable of focusing on one thing at a time. And the part of your brain that chooses what you focus on is called the *Reticular Activating System*. You program what the RAS focuses on through intention and emotion. Sharing with your client that this is the part of the brain that you are training in this exercise can be very beneficial to know.

- This exercise can be very challenging at first, but with time your client will get better at turning on their imagination and visualizing at a powerful level.

- Have your client pendulate back and forth between their anchor memory and their future event until they are visualizing this future event through the lens of their desired expansive emotion.

- This exercise can trigger a client's parasympathetic nervous system. Make sure that you are always reminding them to take deep breaths throughout the visualization to relax their body and mind.

- Make this fun! This is a highly transformative tool!

How to Truly Manifest Your Desires: Increase Your Vibration and Fulfill Your Life Purpose

By Ditte Young

Manifesting what you want can feel like a struggle. You might be discouraged that your life isn't the way it should be, despite your best efforts. This exercise helps you manifest the greatest good in your life when it comes to your relationships, finances, work, and everything that has an impact on your life and well-being.

Great for:

- Anyone who believes in manifestations but has difficulties creating what they want.

- People who often find themselves suffering or stuck with persistent negative emotions.

- Spiritual workers who want to widen their insight into how the Universe really works.

You've probably heard it before, and I'll tell it to you again: the Universe doesn't work against you. It works for you! The Universe will always try to evolve you to be the best version of yourself. If you let it, it will help you to become loving in a way where you no longer care about what other people do to you. You will want to help others, simply because you can.

This isn't easy, however. It's a long journey getting there since we all have an ego that wants recognition, justice, self-preservation, power, self-confidence, and other skills that suit our self-defense mechanisms in order to survive in the world.

I believe that you are born with a karma lesson. I believe in regression and past lives too. I have experienced it too many times to ignore the fact that we carry around stories, emotions, and beliefs that really don't make any sense if we only investigate the lives and childhoods we had in this life.

The karma lesson is a form of contract all of us have agreed upon in between our lives as human beings. We carry a responsibility in the things that are happening for us because we have asked for the lesson. We haven't asked for the details. The lessons come in many detailed forms if you choose to look at them like that instead of viewing life as something that is trying to get you down. We are told that we can only experience what we are capable of handling.

As a mother to a multi-handicapped child, I must say that I found it very difficult to accept this. Regardless of the traumatizing things we experience in life, there will always be a greater cause in the end. Time is fluid in the spiritual world, so it can take 1000 years before the lesson is learned and the karma is solved for one soul. These unresolved energies from previous lives will come into our present life one way or another.

Energy will always repeat itself if it isn't released. Read that again! This is exactly the reason why many people find they go into a loop, or they keep experiencing the same things, drama, or problems in their lives. They haven't found a way to get around it. Human beings are the most addictive creatures. When we experience a situation, our brain will store it and assume that next time we find ourselves in the same situation or something similar, the same emotion will occur.

When you think about a situation, you create emotions. The emotions will send a message to your brain and organs, which will produce hormones like adrenalin and will start a chain reaction with the neurotransmitters that you are not aware of. These reactions then lead to your behaviors and, ultimately, create the same outcome.

We have two energies that are inside of us and around us:

1) The light and love

2) The darkness and fear

One energy can't live without the other one. They are bound to find a balance to evolve us, and if you resist this balance, you will experience a constant inner conflict in what you do. As soon as they find balance, the next level occurs to make you develop into a loving person with less ego and greater heart.

Manifesting your inner desires requires you have a balance between the light and the darkness inside of you and around you.

Regardless of everything you want and desire, you must become aware and accept that the universe will always know the higher purpose or what's best for you, since your perspective can't be as elevated. You can't see the same things when you are standing on the ground in your house as the pilot in an airplane flying miles above your house, watching the landscape around you. You also must accept that you cannot wish or manifest something for another person. They have their individual journey and karma lessons, and you are not powerful enough to interfere with it. You can have an impact on other people but can never control their journey.

Steps to practice:

1. **Write down the things you want in your life**
   Visualize them as if they are already in your present life. Find the emotions you would feel when you have what you want. For example, you may have written down:
   "I wish for a girlfriend or boyfriend, so I don't feel lonely anymore"
   "I wish for a bigger house, so I am able to breathe and feel freedom in my own home"
   "I wish for a raise of XX dollars a month, so I am able to provide things to my family"

2. **Read your manifestations and then find the emotion you *want* to attract**
   Try finding the positive emotion instead of the negative. Instead of avoiding feeling lonely, look for a more positive feeling. What is the opposite of that? Loved?

3. **Write down your manifestation again but wish for the emotion first**
   This could be:
   "I wish to feel loved and find a soulmate"
   "I wish for freedom and space"
   "I wish for me and my family to always have enough"

When you wish for happiness, bliss, true love, and freedom, the universe will send it back to you very fast because you are wanting positive emotions, not material things you believe your happiness relies on.

Do this on a regular basis and you will constantly see that you already have the things you are wishing for. Regardless of if it is you or a client. All human beings are striving to reach more, make more, and receive more because we are hungry for development and challenges to stimulate the cognitive part of our brain.

You can live a life in abundance, and you already have it. It is entirely up to us what we choose every day when we meet an obstacle or a problem. Are we thankful for the lessons or are we determined to suffer from them? Whatever we focus on we will receive more of that energy.

I know what I choose. I hope you do the same and will pass it on.

PART 4
GET IT DONE:

STRATEGIES FOR TAKING MORE ACTION

The Art of Taking Action and Sprinting Towards Your Dreams
By Ian Griffith

It's so easy to dream about what we want, and it's so hard to take action. We all have resistance to change and growth because the emotions of fear, distraction, and procrastination keep us from our destiny. This exercise uncovers the art of taking action using proven strategies and methodologies that work for the top companies in the world.

Great for:

- Accomplishing a particular project or goal when you're having trouble getting started.

- Overcoming distraction, overwhelm, and fear to achieve big goals.

- Those with a great desire to transform their lives, but who haven't found a strategy that works.

- Leading your team, clients, or a group you coach in taking more action towards goals.

In my teenage years, I started writing about my life's biggest dreams and goals in a journal. Some of my dreams were very ambitious for me at that time. I wanted to be an author, a speaker, a coach, and a leader. I also wanted to leave a legacy for the world and to help others who followed after me.

The thought of working on my dreams was inspiring and motivating. However, I would freeze every time I felt myself about to take action. I would say to myself, "I'll do it later when I have more time, resources, wisdom, and courage."

I promised myself that I would go after these dreams later in life when the time was right. The truth is, there was a tremendous amount of fear holding me back. I should have known that I was making a huge mistake. I ended up forgetting about most of my dreams altogether.

Instead of following my dreams, I got a degree in technology and rose through the ranks to director level. I was able to work at many of the top companies in the world. However, I had a deep feeling of incompleteness inside. I was not living my dream. I had forgotten what my true purpose was. I had achieved so much, and yet I was unfulfilled.

It was decades later when I found my journal filled with dreams I had never taken action on.

When I read all of my unfulfilled promises, I realized I hadn't lived my life's true purpose for much of my life. Immediately, I knew that these dreams in my journal were very much still alive in my heart and my soul. This journal held the key to my true destiny and fulfillment.

I felt a wave of fear as I imagined myself finding this journal when I was eighty years old and realizing then why my entire life felt unfulfilled. Suddenly, the fear of living an unlived life was greater than the fear of moving toward my dreams. That was the moment I made a powerful oath. 'I will take action on my dreams, no matter what.'

Once I started taking action towards my dreams, my life became so much better. I was so grateful for the avalanches of abundance that poured into every area of my life. During this awakening, I also found that I loved to contribute to others. It became my mission to help others make their dreams come true as well. I created workshops, seminars, coaching programs, masterminds, and more. I built everything with one purpose: to help others overcome the fear mindset that stops us all. My mission was to do whatever it takes to encourage people to run towards their dreams and positively transform their life in whatever way possible.

So I set up all kinds of systems to help motivate people to go after their dreams. My clients were so ready to take action by the end of our coaching sessions. They would promise to move forward toward their goals, projects, and dreams by the next time we met. However, there was a problem. When I checked in with them the following week, my clients had made no progress.

When I dug deeper, I found my clients shared common reasons for failing to act towards their dreams. "There were too many things to do," "Something with a higher priority came up," "The dream became overwhelming," or "The time just flew by with no clear deadline." Even though my clients wanted to accomplish their goals, they couldn't bring themselves to take action with their current strategies.

It was at this moment when I came upon one of life's greatest truths. Mindset, motivation, and enthusiasm are never enough. We must master the art of taking action to reach our dreams. So I started on a quest to find a solution to the problem. What system, structure, or strategy could I create to ensure those I coach take consistent, focused, and massive action?

Over the last decade, I have been the acting director at many of the greatest technology companies in the world. The methods I've employed have turned companies around and made a difference for hundreds of employees across dozens of teams. I help world-class, billion-dollar companies plan, take action on, and achieve their projects. I do this by breaking their projects into bite-size pieces named sprints.

By breaking large tasks into sprint-sized pieces, we allow our teams to be successful every two weeks. We measure those pieces completed, and we celebrate their work.

Team sprinting works remarkably well as there is less time for teams to get distracted, overwhelmed, or give up. Once the team completes their sprint, they celebrate crossing the finish lines and discuss their wins. *Stopping to celebrate small wins keeps motivation high and drives enormous productivity.*

One day, the answer came to me. I would use my experience in leading company teams and create a system that achieved the same outstanding outcomes for individuals. I could create a smaller version, or a micro-version, of sprinting sessions for individuals. These sprinting sessions would only be 25 to 45 minutes, but would incorporate all the benefits these companies enjoyed. Micro-sprinting was born. It became the de facto way we got important projects done.

I started taking my clients, and teams, through micro-sprinting sessions, and the results amazed them. Since then, I've led hundreds of micro-sprinting sessions for thousands of people. During these sessions, people have been able to take action on dreams they never would believe they could achieve. In fact, three of my clients went through micro-sprinting sessions to write chapters in this very book. I've given micro-sprinting sessions to clients, influencers, coaches, teams, companies, and executives. Everyone who has taken part has consistently achieved outstanding results. I know that when you use the exercise below, any dream, no matter how big it is, can become a reality.

For action to be effective in micro-sprinting sessions, the following things need to happen:

1. **Limit the amount of WIP (Work in Progress) to just one task.** You cannot take action when you multitask. Many studies have proven that we are ineffective and incapable of producing quality work unless we focus on our efforts. Ask any juggler, and they will tell you, the fewer pins in the air, the easier it is.

2. **Limit the amount or scope of our work.** By limiting the scope, you can stay motivated and focused. Limiting the scope also keeps overwhelming feelings at a distance by breaking your most significant dreams into sprint-sized objectives. Take larger goals and break them down to sprint size pieces.

   (Note: If you need help to break down your goals, you can go to http://www.microsprinting.com to get specific steps needed to achieve this aim.)

3. **Use a timer to limit the time you focus on your goal.** A short time limit ensures you focus and work for the entire sprint session. You don't have any time to waste on procrastinating, feeling overwhelmed, or getting distracted. Through hundreds of micro-sprinting sessions, we have found that the 25-45 minute threshold is best to stay focused.

Even though it is possible to conduct micro-sprinting sessions solo, I suggest you go through these action steps with at least one other person. Here are some reasons micro-sprinting in groups works so well:

1. **The sprint commitment** - Everyone takes a few minutes beforehand to tell the others about the work they are committed to accomplishing during the sprint. This reinforces their focus and resolve before taking action.

147

2. **The time pressure** - A timer is set and runs for the duration of the sprint, in view of everyone. There is a kind of excitement that comes from knowing everyone is racing to complete their sprint goal.

3. **The teamwork** - Going after big dreams is more fun when everyone works together. It's much easier to move forward while being supported by a positive peer group. As a team, there is a desire to keep up and a pressure to take action together so everyone can rise together.

4. **The peer pressure** - Micro-sprinting creates a friendly and exciting competition. As the timer ticks down, who is going to get the most done?

5. **The deadline** - It is in our nature to procrastinate, so there is significant power in this immediate deadline. When a deadline looms close, everyone keeps their focus. There is no time for distraction or thinking about unimportant things.

6. **The review** - There is a brief review at the end of each sprint. Everyone shares the accomplishments achieved during this session. The anticipation of sharing as time ticks down motivates people to achieve their sprint commitments and make exceptional results happen.

7. **The celebration** - The session is over. It's time to celebrate! Share appreciation for the work done, and talk about big dreams. Other ways to celebrate are to play music, share wins, or even brag a little. Celebrating wins early and often reinforces productive work and brings up morale.

So now, let's get to the exact steps to follow in this exercise.

1. **Schedule the micro-sprinting session** - With friends, peers, members from a micro-sprinting group, or even yourself. Each session is timed and can be 25-45 minutes long. Usually, teams conduct micro-sprinting sessions on zoom or an equivalent platform. Mirco-sprinting is even better when a group meets in person.

2. **Plan the micro-sprinting session** - Everyone meets on zoom, and the sprint planning begins. One member sets a timer for 5 minutes. During these five minutes, each person announces what they want to accomplish in the upcoming micro-sprint to the group.

3. **Begin the micro-sprinting session** - One member sets a timer on their phone for 25-45 minutes, and the sprinting begins. Everyone works on their sprint commitment, and their zoom camera is on. (Pro-tip: I usually play non-lyrical movie soundtracks during the sprint to make the experience more intense, creative, and entertaining.)

4. **End the micro-sprinting session** - When the session timer goes off, the music is turned down, and the review begins. To conduct the review, one member sets a timer for 5 minutes. During these 5 minutes, everyone tells the group what they accomplished. Then, the group compares it against the initial sprint commitment.

5. **Celebrate your wins** - Once the review is over, everyone in the group takes a minute and celebrates. When we celebrate our wins, we condition ourselves to be focused and take action. Anyone who is going toward their dreams and mastering the art of taking action deserves congratulations.

6. **Kick-off a new micro-sprint** - Start steps 2-4 again for as many sprints as the group can accomplish. Go up in

working sprint time if everyone can keep focus for longer micro-sprinting sessions.

7. **End the micro-sprints for the day** - As the micro-sprinting ends for the day, there is a final review. Everyone shares what they accomplished across all the sessions. Before everyone leaves, take a moment to celebrate and schedule the next event.

Great job! You have now mastered the art of taking action, and you are sprinting towards your dreams. Now go to http://www.microsprinting.com to get advanced lessons, worksheets coaching, and opportunities to work with other micro-sprinters who take action towards their dreams, just like you.

Wouldn't It Be Amazing... ?
Deepen Motivation & Vision for Your Big Goals
By Karen Darke

Wouldn't it be amazing if you could live out your deepest dreams? This exercise sets out a simple process to help you overcome your current circumstances, however challenging, so you can envision a pathway toward your big goals. You'll learn how to reframe your negative thoughts and build up the belief to achieve your 'impossible' vision.

Great for:

• Bringing some flames to the kindling of your big goals and ideas.

• Connecting more deeply with your intrinsic motivation for moving forward.

• Finding more inspiration to help fuel your ability to take action.

• Developing positive beliefs and possibility thinking.

When I lay in a hospital bed for months, my neck broken and my body recently paralyzed in a climbing accident, friends stuck a poster of the Himalayas on the ceiling. At first, I felt sadness and frustration. How could I ever go there? How was it possible to experience the true feel of the mountains when I couldn't even walk? I was stuck in a sense of loss and grief for what I could no longer do.

Will was a dear climbing friend, and he helped me navigate the early days of paralysis. On his visits to me in the hospital, his empathic ways always made me feel helped and understood. A few months after my own accident though, he lost his life in a climbing accident. His departure from the world led me to see things very differently. It helped me shift my focus to what I had to be grateful for, and to what I could do, not what I couldn't. The impact of his death transformed my perspective, and I arrived at the first use of the powerful question, "Wouldn't It Be Amazing... ?" (WIBA for shorthand).

"Wouldn't it be amazing to travel through the Himalayas on a handcycle, and truly experience the mountains?"

Three years later I was cycling through Central Asia and across the Himalayas with three friends. I was filled with excitement for the adventure, fused with a good level of fear about the physical and mental obstacles involved with such a long, remote wilderness journey and the extra complications of paralysis in such an environment.

It had started with just a tiny thought: "Wouldn't it be amazing to..." I found three friends willing to join, but had to work hard not to be discouraged by other people's responses to our planned adventure through Central Asia. Comments like "It's a crazy idea," "How on earth will you manage?" "Is it safe?" or "It sounds impossible" were common. We can all shine a light on our own or others' ideas, but equally, we can drain the life out of them by allowing negative thoughts to reign. This was my first lesson in the power of 'flipping' negative thinking and of choosing to listen to those around me that were radiating possibility rather than focusing on all of the potential reasons not to go ahead. I flipped the negative thinking by reframing it and addressing the negative thoughts to help with better planning and risk-reduction on my trip.

From Kashgar at the western edge of China, the 'highway' was a dirt track with occasional herds of sheep. It crossed the Taklamakan Desert. Cycling was dry, dusty, and almost unbearably hot, so we were glad to leave the plains and begin winding slowly upwards toward the giant sand-dune mountains of the Pamir. The only campsites we could find were roadside gravel and sandpits. Brown water churned through the canyons, no sign of anything green amongst the scree and towers of rock.

The mountains were bigger than anything I could have imagined. We were inching through them on the 'The Green Beast', my affectionate name for the large almost four-meter long tandem which I pedaled with my hands at the front. It was like a double-deck chair, my friend in a similarly reclined position behind me and pedaling with his legs. My wheelchair wheels were balanced on the rack at the back of the bike, and the frame of the wheelchair sat in a small trailer behind my friend's regular mountain bike.

Weeks of cycling into thinning air and headwinds were beginning to take their toll as we worked slowly onward and upward towards the high summits. We envied the occasional cyclist we met traveling in the opposite direction, apparently cruising downhill for hundreds of kilometers, though of course, they'd put in the work to get the reward. We had that to look forward to.

"We should reach the top today," I announced to no-one in particular, perhaps surprised myself that we had almost reached the final pass of this incredible cycle through the Western Himalaya. Steep, rocky brown slopes rose steeply, curtains of scree plummeting from ice-cream mountain tops. As we pedaled higher, we passed camels grazing on the greener slopes of a glacier snout. Our stomachs rumbled with hunger. We were running on empty, our last boiled eggs and stale doughballs devoured the previous evening. It didn't seem to matter. The scenery compensated for any hardship.

Our muscles burned and my head became set into a sideways tilt, a sure sign of effort. My hands were numb as the piercing cold penetrated the thin fabric gloves and my breath came short and sharp, the thin air of altitude painful. False summit led to false summit, the mountain contours hiding bends and dog-legs in the road so that the top of the pass seemed to get ever further away, but the glacier-draped peaks appeared smaller; we were getting closer.

Eventually, the gradient slackened and we could see the summit plaque. "The Khunjerab Pass," I almost whispered, the name itself exotic and full of mystery to me. As I looked around at the panorama of giant summits that crammed the sky, dramatic rocky tops jutting into the clouds, and lower slopes plummeting into the Indus Gorge, I felt my cheeks wet with tears. In my wildest dreams, I could never have imagined being there during those months lying in bed with a broken back, only polystyrene ceiling tiles for a view.

We began our descent, leaving the views of the high pass, and plunged into the hairpin road downhill, our tires barely clinging to the rubble-strewn switchbacks. For a moment, I closed my eyes and felt the air tickling against my skin and smelt the pure high air. I had dreamt of this feeling and I had grieved for it also. The intensity at which I felt alive was dialed up. What I was doing physically had changed, but the experience was brighter, the texture richer.

I recently discovered that "Khunjerab" in the native language is spelled "Khun-zerav," which literally means "bloodstream." Cycling over it was representative of what flows in my own bloodstream: a passion for journeys, wild places, and cycling. What is in your bloodstream? What is one of your big WIBA's? What are you excited about creating? Is there something that would be surprising and special for you to achieve, but seems a bit far from reach?

Exploring our "WIBA's" is a fun and special way to help bring goals and dreams into reality. Our mind loves imagery. Conjuring with our relaxed mind, we can see and experience beyond the logic and mechanics of our cognitive brain, engaging our subconscious and emotive brain with our big goals and dreams. We connect with all our senses and invoke a more powerful inner drive.

"Our mind is not a vessel to be filled, but a fire to be kindled." – Plutarch

A WIBA at first is just an idea, and is very vulnerable at this stage. When we begin to share it with other people, their concerns or fears can be like pouring water on the struggling flames. It is important to nurture and tend to your WIBA like a new fire. At the kindling stage of your WIBA, it matters to spend time with people that add energy to your ideas rather than dampening the flames. Ideas are the kindling of life. They need to be tended to carefully. Nurture the sparks to make the flames that lead you to the roaring fire.

Once your WIBA gains momentum, it may be helpful to break it down and explore the elements that help you bring it alive.

Steps:

W: What

I: Inspiration

B: Belief

A: Action

What? Get really clear about what you are aiming for and why it matters to you – how does it connect to 'deeper' you, your values, and drivers.

Inspiration? Feeling inspired is like fuel to our spirit, so consider your sources of inspiration to keep moving towards your WIBA: time with other people, nature, visualization, connection to the emotion behind things?

Belief? How 'wild' does this WIBA seem from reality and so what is your current level of belief? Our belief and confidence rise when we notice the small steps and wins along the way, so acknowledge and recognize the progress you are making. Acknowledge and support a growing inner belief, rather than feeding the thoughts of doubt or imposter.

Action? What are the stepping-stones towards the big WIBA? Break down the small steps that you need to take to get from where you are to where you want to be. Call on help, ask questions, research, connect and explore to help define those steps.

I hope you like this concept of having a WIBA. Run free with your vision and follow the steps to creating amazing things.

Tips for coaches:

- A WIBA can be of any scale, micro- to macro-, short-term to longer-term. Mine have ranged from learning to sit up in bed without the use of my abdominals, to pushing my first 10km, to big-scale adventures like the one described.

- Tune into your client and help them explore their passion, curiosity, and dreams. What ideas or possibilities seem to light them up, and how could these be translated into a WIBA?

- Help your client through this process, engaging first the conscious thinking brain.

- Build on this by helping your client into a more relaxed state, ideally with their eyes closed, helping them visualize and connect to images of their WIBA and the steps of the process.

- Encourage your client to use all senses - to connect with what they can see, hear, touch, how they are moving and feeling, who is with them or not, what is around them in the environment, etc.

- Suggest the client repeat the exercise for themselves when in their most relaxed state of non-busy-beta-brain-waves e.g. on waking, or just before sleeping.

- The client can use any images or anchors that arise through the exercise to strengthen the connection to their WIBA going forward, e.g. a snapshot in their mind / a new screensaver / a physical posture / a photo or image, etc.

The Art of Being Awkward: Take Social Risks and Grow Your Capacity to Connect
By Glenn Valentin

This exercise teaches you how to move past your fears and insecurities to create meaningful connections with strangers. Not only will these new acts of bravery give you an adrenaline rush, but with practice, they will also grow your capacity to act courageously, stretch your comfort zone, and follow your dreams. A bonus: reaching out to people you don't yet know will also brighten their day.

Great for:

- Improving social skills and building confidence in talking to strangers.

- Warming up before a date, sales talk, or social event.

- Introverts who want to challenge themselves.

- Cultivating a deeper sense of connection with other people.

- Those who enjoy the feeling of adrenaline and excitement of doing something new.

I follow her down the road and steadily close the original 30-meter gap between her and my belly full of butterflies. Halfway down the approach, as I'm preparing myself to say hello, she takes a turn left and steps into a shop. I freeze, not knowing what to do.

For the last four days, I have been pushing the limits of my comfort zone far beyond what I had ever believed was possible. With the help of a coach, I have reached out and connected with strangers while riding my bike and paddling a kayak. I have approached women shopping with their friends or strolling in the company of their parents. In all these situations, I had experienced moments of extreme discomfort and been the initiator of some of the most cringeworthy conversations you could imagine. But I'd never had to do this before.

I wonder, 'Is this the glass ceiling of my courage?' Is this a step too far out of my comfort zone? My coach joins me at the entrance of the shop, and starts singing teasingly "Go Glééén, go Glééénnn." I tell him I'm not sure whether I can do this.

I take a couple of deep breaths, delivering just enough oxygen to let the right chemicals flow to the courage-center of my brain. Then I step into the lingerie shop and blush: "Hi, I saw you walking in the street over there. I know this is a bit awkward, but you look stunning and I wanted to introduce myself."

The woman introduces herself as Ellen, and my unexpected appearance makes her laugh. We have a short but enjoyable chat, and she gives me her phone number and agrees to go on a date sometime.

If my life was a Disney movie, I would have lived together with Ellen happily ever after. But my life isn't a Disney movie, so that didn't happen. Even though we kept in touch and tried to find an opportunity to meet up, the logistics of living too far from each other made it impossible for us to go on a date.

Even though that one interaction didn't conclude the exact way I wanted, I learned so much about myself and the power of leaning into our awkwardness. I learned that risking looking foolish can give us the courage to do brave things we never dreamed would be possible. And I'm sure that Ellen - and the bemused shop assistant - will never forget our slightly romantic, slightly awkward moment.

These acts of embracing my awkwardness to approach women helped build my capacity to do many other things that I couldn't have previously imagined I'd be capable of doing. I climbed up the Col du Tourmalet, a famous mountain pass from the Tour de France, on a spacehopper (in case you don't know what this is, it's a large rubber ball you sit on and use to hop forward). If I would have been afraid to look awkward, I'd never have taken up this challenge. And although many people along the road indeed gave me strange looks, I had already developed my ability to take action without being stopped by the judgments or opinions of other people. I raised over €500 for charity, and my feat was covered by national media in five countries. Many people thanked me for bringing something funny in the newspaper in the midst of the Covid-19 outbreak. Later that year, I became the world's first person to cross a mountain range (the Pyrenees) with a unicorn.

Tim Ferriss' *The 4-hour Workweek* introduces the concept of social freedom exercises – practices to do in social situations that help you feel less impacted by other people's opinions or reactions. This way, you learn to make choices aligned with your heart, instead of what society demands of you. My awkwardness exercises build upon this idea, by embracing the discomfort of putting myself in potentially embarrassing situations in order to grow beyond my comfort zone. My twist on social freedom is to take action when you believe it will add to the positive energy of the people around you, not just to benefit yourself.

Luckily, you don't have to go as crazy as climbing up a mountain on a spacehopper right away (or at all). *The Art of Being Awkward* exercise is an easy drill that you can do anywhere there are people, at any time, and without any equipment. I've also used it to go dancing in the streets of Brussels and asking strangers what their dreams in life are.

Steps:

These are the steps for how to approach a stranger and build your capacity to make new connections with people. You could also easily use this method at a business networking event. The secret is to not attach to getting the outcome (or goal) you want and, instead, focus on building the skill (in this case to connect with a stranger). You can adapt this method for any skill you'd like to develop.

1. Go to a place where many people gather, e.g. a town square or shopping mall. Give yourself 1-1.5 hours to do the complete exercise.

2. Start by giving compliments 'in your head' to 20 strangers. Observe people from a distance, and say to yourself what you like about them. This is a warm-up for the actual exercise.

3. Now, you will give actual compliments to 10 strangers you're crossing or walking past. Give the compliment freely, without any need to follow up. Don't force a conversation on the person, but, of course, don't resist the opportunity to enter an interesting conversation if the other person initiates one.

4. The next step is to give compliments to 5 strangers and try to get in a conversation with them. You could start by saying, "You have a beautiful dress, what is your name?" or "You look like a very cheerful person, is that right?"

5. If you have a good conversation going, try to move beyond the small talk pretty quickly. Ask a question such as "What are your dreams in life?", "Are you happy?" or "What does a perfect day in your life look like?" Your aim here is to practice connecting to strangers on a deeper level. Use this opportunity to really get to know the other person.

6. If you have a great connection with that person and feel the genuine desire to see him/her again, then suggest that you exchange contact details. They may even ask you for your number or email.

Tips for coaches or people who want to try this out on their own:

• Don't force yourself to give compliments 'because you have to do the exercise'. Be genuine, you have to mean what you're saying. The indicated amount of compliments is only a guideline, the intention behind them is more important.

• Going from step 1 to step 2 might be too much of a leap. As a smoother progression, you might start by saying "hello" or nod at people.

• You can increase the fun-factor of this exercise by finding a social freedom buddy. This way, your fear gets turned into excitement very rapidly.

- When doing social freedom exercises with clients, it's important to know their background, their level of social easiness, social skills, self-confidence, and fear. Progress *The Art of Being Awkward* practices accordingly.

By practicing an exercise like this, I've noticed that I've become much more at ease in social situations. Doing sales talks, going on a first date, or starting a conversation with people at a party causes me less stress because I have been training my 'social courage muscle' via *The Art of Being Awkward* exercises.

On top of that, it has helped me to have fewer judgments about strangers. How often do we see someone and judge what they're like without getting to know them? But by actually stepping into a conversation with a stranger, you almost inevitably discover something beautiful about him/her and discover you have more in common than you'd expected based on your initial impression. In my experiences, this has helped me be less judgmental, establish more empathy and see a bit of myself in everyone I encounter.

7 Steps To Take Now To Grow Your Small Business
By Paul Cantrell

Many small business owners get overwhelmed or feel stuck on how to grow their businesses. Focused on the day-to-day of running the business, they don't feel like they have the time to work on growing it. This exercise provides some simple yet very important steps you can take to start growing your business quickly.

Great for:

- The busy small business owner who is also a full-time operator of their business.

- Those who have tried other approaches to growing their business that haven't worked.

- Those who've been putting off working on their business for a while because they don't know what to focus on first.

I've found that many small business owners jump into creating websites, social media content, paid ads, and promotional emails because they want to quickly start connecting with customers. But they skip some important steps and then wonder why they aren't getting the results they want. To address this, I created this 7-step process to ensure you are working on your goals, role, and really understanding your customers and your target market before creating content to reach customers. I refined this process based on my 20 years of experience as a management consultant working with big companies to help them grow and run their businesses more efficiently.

The best way to follow this process is to do one lesson a day for seven days. Some will take more time than others, but moving through it quickly will help keep up your momentum and your drive to work on your business.

Steps:

1. Making Time

Have you wanted to work on your business for a while but feel like there is never enough time? This is common for most small business owners. For a variety of reasons, we tend to put off these important but not urgent activities. Waiting until tomorrow to work on your business won't make a big difference, but when that happens for weeks and months, then you will most certainly delay meeting your overall business goals. And you will continue working long hours and hoping that things will eventually change.

For your first activity, make a list of all the things you are spending time on during your workday. Be honest and include time on social media, time getting distracted by browsing news or other internet sites, time spent taking breaks, preparing meals, etc. It is estimated that many office workers are only productive 3-4 hours per day due to non-productive distractions.

Look at that list and make a "not-to-do list". This is a list of things you will not spend time on as they are not contributing to your business. For most people, this alone should free up an hour or more a day to help you make time to work on your business.

To ensure you are using this time effectively, you need to schedule it. So go to your calendar right now and schedule the time you will work on the rest of the steps in this lesson. Aim for at least 30 minutes a day, but an hour would be better. If you can only do 3 or 4 days a week, that is fine. Just make sure you schedule the time and commit to yourself that you will focus on the lessons.

2. Setting Goals

Those who write down their goals are significantly more likely to meet them. So take your time today to document your goals for yourself for the next 90 days, 1 year, 5 years, and even 20 years out if you can. Make sure you have personal and business goals.

On the personal side, set goals for your finances such as personal savings and income, and net worth. Also include health-related goals since being healthy and having good energy will be vital to your overall success. Health goals can include weight targets, exercise routines, and diet expectations. And finally, set some relationship goals such as getting new relationships and/or improving existing ones.

For business goals, set financial goals such as revenue, income, and number of customers. Also, set goals for your role in the business. For example, in 5 years do you want to be still involved in the day-to-day business, or are you more of an owner spending less time per week? You should also set some goals around how you want to share your success by giving back to the community (see more in step 6 below).

3. Understanding Your Customers

Can you describe your ideal customer? Most small business owners will answer that question with 'Yes, it is people between the ages of X & Y, with income over $Z'. Maybe they will have some more descriptors, but that is about it.

When I say 'understanding your customers', I mean what scares them, what motivates them, what would make them decide to buy your product or service, what pain and challenges are they feeling that you can address, etc. Really getting into your customers' minds will help you build messaging that will resonate more with them.

For this lesson, write down a detailed description of your ideal customer - include both demographics and what they think about. Then go interview 3-5 of them to refine your understanding.

4. Understanding Your Niche

As you better understand your customer, you also want to refine your niche or target market.

While it may sound contradictory, the more you narrow your target market, the more you can grow your business. You do this by providing messages to your potential clients that resonate with them and make them want to buy from you.

If you continue to chase a broad market you will find that your solutions are not as valuable since they are too general. Also, you will have a hard time standing out in the crowded social media and advertising markets where everyone starts to look the same.

Now, take a look at how you describe your target market and, leveraging what you learned about your customers in Lesson 3, identify some more specific types of customers that you would like to serve in your business. These may be a subset of your existing customers that you enjoy working with the most and get the most value from in your business.

5. Building Your Marketing Strategy

Now that you understand your target market and know exactly what motivates them to buy, you can build your marketing strategy. When people skip these earlier steps and they start marketing to a broad set of customers with general messages and comments, they find that they are not able to attract customers and get them to buy. But by being very clear on who your customers are in a specific market niche, you will start getting more sales and closing more big deals.

First, take a look at your existing products and services and refine them as needed to better meet your customers' needs that you identified in the previous lessons.

Next, create the messages that will get their attention and make them want to buy from you. Clearly describe the pain that they have today, a simple description of how your business solves that, and how much better their life will be after they buy from you.

Find out where your ideal clients are "hanging out" and start sharing your messages there. This may be on social media, online forums, reading local magazines or newspapers, TV, etc. These are the channels that you will want to focus on.

Marketing can be done through paid advertising and free online channels. There are many creative ways to reach your customers. Just think about the niche you are targeting and the challenges you are addressing, and look for methods to share your messages and stories to get their attention.

6. **Your Values, Mission, and Philanthropy**

Everyone gets into business for different reasons, but we should all have a cause bigger than ourselves. You will find that with a greater cause, you will have more success in your business. This is due to having more motivation to succeed and focusing more on finding solutions instead of making excuses when things get tough.

First, document the values for your business. These describe how you treat your employees and customers and how you will make difficult decisions in your business.

Then create a mission statement for your business. This should provide a goal to guide the business over the next few years. Create a poster of your values and mission statement and place it somewhere you will see it every day.

And thirdly, create some philanthropic goals for your business. How will you give back to your community and contribute to those interests that are the most important to your customers? Being able to help others should be a goal of every business owner, so please set some goals around this.

7. Improving Your Mindset

Experts suggest that 80% of success is psychology, and 20% is based on your capabilities. So no matter how much great knowledge you can learn from this and other lessons in this book, you still won't succeed without the right mindset.

As you set goals in lesson 2, you need to believe those are possible. You need to visualize yourself and your business having that level of success or even more.

To help you get your mind in the right state, here are 3 techniques to try:

a. Meditation - if you've never tried it, you can find some great business guided meditations on YouTube. Find a way to clear your mind and use these to help you visualize success in your business. Do this daily if you can, even for only a few minutes.

b. Incantations - In the book 'Think and Grow Rich' by Napoleon Hill, he describes creating a major purpose statement that visually describes how your life will be at some point in the future. And he found that by doing this and reading it passionately multiple times a day, your brain gets trained to believe it will happen, and you will be much more likely to achieve your goals.

c. Priming - Have you ever had something happen one day that didn't bother you at all, and the same thing happens another day that makes you angry? This is because of how our brains are 'primed' ahead of time to interpret events. In the mornings, you can spend 10 minutes thinking about what you are grateful for, sending love out to others, and visualizing something you want to happen that day or in the future. Your brain will automatically interpret situations that day in a more positive light, and you will be more effective in your business

8. Celebrate!

Congratulations on completing these important 7 lessons. If you take the time to really think about these lessons and implement changes in your business, you will start seeing results soon!

Mirror, Mirror on the Wall: Falling in Love With the Person Inside
By Jim McDowell

Gazing at our reflection in the mirror is one of the most powerful things we can do for ourselves. This exercise guides you through a simple 2-minute process for overcoming critical inner voices and connecting with your most authentic self.

Great for:

- Those who want to believe in themselves deeply but need a system to make it happen.

- Falling in love with yourself as you are right now and who you are becoming.

- Coaching others to become greater than they think they are through mirror therapy.

Most homes today have a few standard things in them that we take for granted. Washer and dryer, sinks, kitchens, things you use almost every day. One of the most powerful items you own is that big mirror in your bathroom. Every day, you use it to brush your teeth, brush your hair, put on makeup, and more. When you look in the mirror, what does it show you? How do you see yourself right now? Who is the real you in that mirror?

Growing up, everyone told me I needed to be faster, stronger, bigger, and better. So when I looked into that big mirror in my bathroom, I was always looking for more. When I was in the gym lifting weights, I was always looking at myself in the mirror at a surface level, judging my looks both positively and negatively. I kept seeing that I needed to be more. I told myself I needed to lift more weights and push myself to greater limits. From my childhood onward, I believed I showed my value by being what others wanted me to be. So it became my quest to become the person that others had envisioned. Why couldn't I be comfortable in my own skin? Why did their words rattle around in my head with so much power?

As a Midwestern child growing up in Arkansas, I had dreams of becoming a star athlete in football. I achieved that success at highschool and then at university. I then wanted to become a successful cosmetic dentist. After graduating from dental school in LA, I felt like I had checked off that dream. My private dental practice had many entrepreneurs, celebrities, and professional sports Hall of Famers as patients.

In my quest to always become bigger and better, I decided I wanted to become a professional wrestler. I achieved my goal and since then it's been one amazing ride. I have wrestled and performed in front of thousands while traveling all over this beautiful Earth. There were epic times in wrestling when I beat gigantic men over 7 feet tall and 450 pounds. I fought giants and won, and yet I never felt truly fulfilled. I remember looking at myself in my big bathroom mirror. It was so painful to never feel satisfied with that man looking back at me.

My eyes scoured my mirror each time I stood in front of it, looking for imperfections. I looked for the 'negatives' to fix or perfect instead of reveling in the good there. That quest for perfection has led me to Botox, liposuction, lower blepharoplasty, skin resurfacing, to name a few of the many cosmetic procedures I've done to my body. But we can't have cosmetic procedures inside our brains to change the way we see ourselves.

I often wondered, "Can I ever be comfortable enough to thrive and love myself as the accurate reflection that mirror shows? Do I still value how others see me too much? Should I even believe how others see me? How can I overcome the weight of the naysayers' words that drain me and drag me down?"

One day, as I was looking in the mirror with my thoughts bringing me down, I had a moment of inspiration. I decided I would never again weigh myself down when I looked into my reflection. Instead of just receiving feedback from my critical mind, I would invest in this man in the mirror with my heart. This is the moment everything changed. Now when I looked in the mirror, I did not see a hard stare. I now saw a man who needed compassion, connection, and support. As I continued with my effort, day after day, I saw soul behind my eyes, burning bright. No longer was I stuck focusing on the forever unfulfilled expectations on the outside. I could connect with my soul, my strength, my truth, and my heart. After all these years, I now felt the joy and fulfillment of loving who I am.

Once I healed myself, I knew I wanted to pay this amazing gift of wisdom forward. I began coaching others and teaching them the secrets of mirror therapy. One of my coaching clients is an NFL Hall of Fame coach and is at the top of his profession. Trust is at the crux of any relationship on this scale. This brilliant coach had just spent the Thanksgiving weekend all across NFL games and news conferences. On Monday morning, we met and analyzed everything about his self-image in every situation. We studied his presence in front of the cameras and focused on detailed areas like his smile. We spent the next few weeks in front of his mirror on the wall, following the same steps you are about to learn. By the time he was back in front of cameras, his magnetism had grown exponentially. This coach now radiated with a much higher energized persona. He now *believed* what his eyes told him!

Today's exercise is simple, repeatable, and quickly done daily (or twice daily) at home. We live in such a fast-paced world that we rarely stop and look deep into the person's eyes looking back at us from the mirror. By not slowing down enough to stop and connect with ourselves, we miss out on something incredibly important. What do we yearn for in that gaze into the mirror? A genuine connection to our inner soul and heart.

This mirror exercise will help you to connect more deeply to the true you underneath the criticisms and judgments. It's time to see yourself in a new way and break through into a brand new, authentic vision of yourself. Let the fun begin.

Steps:

1. Begin by becoming utterly naked in your bathroom. How does that feel? *Know* that it is perfectly normal to be naked. Become comfortable there.

2. Now, take a quick cursory look at the whole you. What do you see? Is what you see the *real* you?

   Before starting your morning off hastily rushing and getting put together for the day, the next 2 minutes will change your life forever.

3. Set a timer and let the deeply connected you look into the mirror. You will lean forward toward the mirror and

deeply gaze into the middle of your eyes. Do not deflect your eyes from your deeply in-tune stare.

4. Intensely feel that connection. Love yourself and who you are. Tell yourself as you continue that gaze that you love *you* and want the best day ever to happen today. Positive affirmations build up self-worth and esteem.

5. Praise yourself out loud. Speak openly and positively about your looks. Look for the positive, not the in-grained negative put-downs from family and friends. Do they mean well, or are they jealous? You are now becoming a new creature. A beast with immortal beauty and strength.

6. Please go on, do it! Try this simple exercise to begin and end your day, and you will see your belief in yourself grow more and more every day.

"Mirror, Mirror on the wall, who is this new person I see and am becoming?" These 2 minutes are *all about you*! The new, positively beautiful, and radiant reflection that you now see externally will grow into the brand new you internally. It's time to live and love you!

As far as my ongoing work in front of my mirror, it's always a work in progress. I still sometimes get stuck in a pattern that doesn't serve me. I ask myself questions such as, "Am I worthy of the accolades that come my way? Am I strong enough to continue to improve myself into a more powerful and endearing persona? Do I believe what my newly calibrated eyes tell me?." Yes, I now know that after a long time of this amazing mirror technique, a new vision is just around the corner.

The Art of Managing Your Mind: Overcome Resistance to Chasing Your 'Impossible' Dreams
By Diane Hopkins

The negative voices in your head are the biggest challenge you'll ever need to overcome if you have big dreams or goals you want to achieve. This exercise gives you a simple method for dealing with those inner demons, so you'll know exactly how to find better thoughts, handle negativity, and create your own motivation for taking action.

Great for:

- Those who have big dreams that seem unrealistic or impossible.

- Those who struggle with self-doubt, procrastination, or not following through on their own goals.

- Generating the motivation to take action toward big goals when success isn't always guaranteed.

As a writing coach, I've frequently observed in my clients how much our thoughts can influence our success – or sabotage it. So often, we are our own biggest enemy. Despite our dreams to write a book, start a business or become an international speaker, we tend to find ourselves falling back into negative thoughts. Essentially, we talk ourselves out of chasing our big dreams.

What we don't realize is: when we set out to do something new, big, or different, our brains will offer us thoughts *against* doing it. We'll decide it's unrealistic, that we're not skilled enough to do it, and that it simply isn't worth the effort to even try. These thoughts are the 'wet blanket' that kills dreams before we can take the actions necessary for our success.

My writing clients are often surprised when this happens. Their initial enthusiasm for starting their book makes them believe that negative thoughts will never come. And when these thoughts do arrive, they worry that something has gone wrong. If writing doesn't always feel good and 100% inspired, then maybe they shouldn't be writing a book after all. The negative voice turns into doubt and they start to question whether they can achieve their dream.

But the answer to this problem is to expect resistance from your brain. Don't be surprised when you feel discouraged or experience doubt when embarking on a new project or vision for your life. This is normal. Know that these negative thoughts will come and learn how to manage them so they don't stop you from pursuing your goals.

The tricky thing about these negative thoughts is that they have you believing they're true. But your thoughts don't necessarily reflect reality. Ironically, often clients with a lot of natural writing talent have the thought that they're not a good enough writer. Even though they may also believe, at times, that they *do* have writing talent, this negative thought still pops up and stops them from wanting to keep writing. Having a negative thought doesn't make it true. But they can be dangerous because they just might convince you to walk away from your dream.

Practicing fake positivity won't help. It's like when someone compliments you on your outfit the day you've left the house feeling you look awful. You act defensive and swat away their compliment because you just don't believe it. And if you don't believe in your positive thoughts or affirmations, they can actually create more resistance. You decide you want to think, "I look great" but you don't really believe it. So you end up having a debate in your head. Because the negative thoughts are often stronger, you'll defend that position by giving your brain lots of evidence to support it. I don't look good because I didn't bother to iron my shirt today and I didn't have time to blow-dry my hair and... Your brain will keep coming up with reasons to validate the negative thought.

Your brain is a master at collecting evidence. When you have a negative thought about your ability to achieve your dream, you will scan your life for evidence that it's true. For example, if you want to write a book, you'll only notice writers you think are better than you. You'll only pay attention to blogs talking about how difficult it is to get published. You'll only hear people say they prefer Netflix to reading books. If you're not careful, you'll wind up convincing yourself that what you deeply desire is out of reach.

Even worse, because we subconsciously look for evidence that a negative thought is true, without realizing what we're doing, we end up creating a self-fulfilling prophecy. When we think negatively about *our* ability to achieve a goal or the odds *anyone* has to achieve it, then we will undoubtedly feel discouraged. When we feel discouraged, we won't take the actions required to make our dream a success. If we think it's hard to get published, we won't get up and write in the mornings. We won't ever bother finishing our book, because what's the point? And then our result will be never having our book published, not because it's too hard, but because we never showed up enough to finish it.

The solution is to manage the negative thoughts we inevitably will have, and find more positive ones that will serve us in accomplishing our goals. We need to embrace thoughts that will fuel our efforts and motivate us to keep going and keep taking action, but we also need thoughts that we can believe. It's no point thinking positively if we're just faking it. If you're able to persuade yourself that you're destined to be an award-winning author, business owner, or international speaker, then that's great. But most of us can't make that leap so easily. Most of us need different kinds of thoughts. And this is exactly what I'll show you how to do.

The exercise that follows gives you a simple process for managing your negative thoughts and finding more positive and believable ways of thinking about your goal. I use the example of someone with the dream of writing a book but you can insert any dream or big goal into this method.

Steps:

1. **Write down a list of all the negative thoughts you have when you think about your impossible dream**

   For example, if you want to write a book, you might have thoughts like:

   It's not realistic.

   Most writers never get published.

   Only really gifted writers get to become authors.

   I don't know where to start.

   Do I really have anything interesting to say that others would want to read?

2. **Spot the stickiest thoughts**

The stickiest thoughts are the ones that bother you the most. They create the strongest feelings of doubt and discouragement. These are the thoughts that can persuade you to give up on your dream.

Go through your list of negative thoughts and circle the one or two that feel the heaviest for you. Often we can push away some negative thoughts like passing clouds but others stay hovering on our horizon, blocking out the sun. These are the ones we need to address and not simply ignore, pretending like they will go away on their own.

3. **Identify the self-fulfilling nature of your stickiest thoughts**

Take your stickiest thoughts and identify, using the questions below, your self-fulfilling prophecy. I've adapted these questions from what The Life Coach School (www.thelifecoachschool.com) refers to as "The Model."

Thought - What is the sticky thought?

Emotion - What emotion does this thought create in you?

Action/Inaction - What do you then do or not do?

Result - What is the end result?

For example, if your dream is to write a book, your stickiest thought might be:

Thought - I'm not that good of a writer.

Emotion - I feel discouraged.

Action/Inaction - I don't write regularly. I don't show my writing to others for feedback. I don't seek help to develop my writing skills. When I do write, I criticize myself and always look for the weaknesses.

Result - I don't improve as a writer.

You can see in this example how the thoughts you have will end up creating your result. You'll prove yourself right by not taking the actions you need to become the person capable of living your dream.

This step is really important because it will show you how much you are creating your own reality. And it will also give you hope that by adopting new thoughts, you'll also create new emotions and actions, and, most importantly, a new result.

4. **Pick a new thought that will serve your dream**

   When picking a new thought, you need to find one that you can believe. It's no use trying to convince yourself, "I'm an amazingly gifted writer" when you've been thinking "I'm not that good of a writer." If you pick a new thought that's too positive compared to the old one, you risk getting in a tug-of-war in your head between the two thoughts. And, because you've been thinking the old thought for longer, that's the one that'll win.

   Instead, come up with a thought that's *more* positive *and* that you can believe. For example:

   I'm a pretty good writer and I can also improve my skills as a writer.

   Every day that I write, I'm becoming a better writer.

You can see that these thoughts will create emotions that motivate you to take productive action toward achieving your dream. You don't have to believe you're the next Elizabeth Gilbert or Paulo Coello in order to complete your book. You just need to believe you're good enough to write it.

5. Notice when you keep looking for evidence of your old thought

Because of your new thought, you go out and start taking new actions that will help you achieve your dream. You're feeling much more positive and then... boom! Your old negative thoughts return.

Following our previous example, you might go to a writing workshop where you and the other participants are asked to read a short piece of writing out loud to the group for feedback. You listen to the first person and they're good. Too good. "They're a much better writer than me," you think. Once again, that old thought, "I'm not *that good* of a writer" returns. Immediately, you feel discouraged and consider giving up.

6. Reframe your thoughts about this situation

You might be tempted to turn the thought around and try to think the opposite.

I'm a gifted writer. I'm a better writer than them.

But this type of thinking rarely gets you anywhere. You'll keep flip-flopping in your head. Instead of trying to cover up a negative thought with a positive one, like in step 4, find a thought that applies to this situation that you *can* believe.

Some thoughts you could think instead:

They are a good writer and I'm also a good writer.

You can see here how using *and* is a useful way of coming up with new thoughts that will serve your dreams.

Or:

I can learn how to improve my writing by listening to other writers.

They've probably done more writing than I have, and I'll also get better the more I write.

7. **Write down your negative thoughts whenever you feel stuck**

   Return to step 1 whenever you're feeling stuck, confused, or unmotivated. These feelings are usually a sign that negative thinking is dominating the thoughts you're having about your goal. Often, we don't even realize we are thinking negatively until we realize it's been days, weeks, or months of inaction.

   You might even like to do this exercise once a week, to keep track of your negative thoughts so you don't find yourself stuck without knowing why. With practice, you'll find that your brain is able to find more positive thoughts organically, without as much effort. You'll have trained your brain to manage negative thoughts and embrace positive, believable ones.

When you're chasing a big goal or dream, managing your thoughts is the best possible investment of your time and energy. No strategies or actions will work without the motivation needed to implement them. Your mind is the most powerful ally you have, so use it in your favor.

AUTHOR DIRECTORY

Matt Adams

Work Stress Expert, Trainer, Speaker, Consultant, and Coach

Website: https://matthewadams.com

Location: Florence, Italy (originally from Australia)

Matt Adams is a work stress expert, trainer, speaker, consultant, and coach.

After suffering severe stress and burnout at 24 while managing two real estate sales teams, the cell-memory of the experience followed him to other jobs, causing him to resign to release the feelings of stress. Then at age 27, he suffered a severe work-related anxiety attack while driving. The next 4 months were the hardest four months of his life where he experienced up to 100 heart palpitations a day along with lightning-shock feelings in his heart. He ended up working in a factory making ladders and was almost fired due to having too many sick days off.

Through discovering or creating various techniques and strategies, Matt's 10-month self-rehabilitation got him to a point where he was ready to return to work in his field of expertise. Since then, Matt has continued to find or develop techniques and strategies to overcome stress and anxiety, and he now has a tool belt of over 50 different techniques and strategies to draw upon for himself and his clients.

Halley Claire Bass

Human Design Readings, Chakra Clearings, 1:1 Spiritual Life & Business Coaching

Website: halleyclairecoaching.com

Facebook: www.facebook.com/halleyclairecoaching

Email: halley.bass@gmail.com

Social Media Handle: @coach_halley

Location: Berlin, Germany

Halley is the CEO of Halley Claire Coaching. Her mission is to help you give yourself permission to be, do, and have exactly what your heart and soul desires. This is a journey of self-discovery, embracing your strengths, acknowledging your challenges, and making steady progress toward creating a life that inspires you to be the best version of yourself.

Halley began her career studying marketing, because at age 18 when starting university she didn't know much about herself. All she knew is that one day, once she realized what she truly wanted to do with her life, she would use her marketing skills and turn her passion into a business. Eighteen years later, Halley is a walking example to others of what it means to live your life not just on what kind of career you should have, or what society expects of you, but what you feel called to do with your time, energy, and what brings you joy.

Alongside many entrepreneurial endeavors such as graphic design, marketing consulting, and business coaching to earn income, Halley also pursued studies in Human Design, energy medicine, as well as yoga, and spirituality. In 2016, she completed a 2-year nature-connection women's initiation in Sonoma County, California, and in 2018, she obtained her Master Certification in Intuition Medicine® from the Academy of Intuition Medicine® in Sausalito, California. She completed her latest training on Human Design readings in The 9-Centers Mentorship with Human Design teacher, Jes Fields.

Halley is much more than just a business coach. She is also an energy healer, artist, singer, spiritual mentor, and nature lover. She has run expressive arts retreats, led group courses and masterminds for women entrepreneurs, and invented many inspiring workshops on topics including energy medicine, spiritual growth, entrepreneurship, and leadership.

Currently, she has taken her location-independent coaching business to Berlin, where she is looking forward to pursuing more of her artistic and musical interests alongside coaching, energy healing, and Human Design readings.

Daniel Brisbon

ICF ACC Certified Coach, Nature-Connected Life Coach, Transformational Wilderness Guide, Professional Downhill Mountain Bike Racer

Website: abovetreelinecoaching.com

Social Media: @abovetreelineofficial

Location: Denver, CO

Daniel is a certified nature-connected life coach through the International Coaching Federation. His focus is on creating transformational change from the inside out while utilizing nature as a co-guide and collaborator to guiding radical transformation and new visions for his clients. He is also an instructor and lead mentor at the school from which he received his training in coaching called the Earth-Based Institute based out of Boulder, CO.

For your **bonus Radical Daydreaming Meditation,** click on this link.

Paul Cantrell

Head Business Coach at The Business Superstars

Website: https://TheBusinessSuperstars.com

Facebook Profile: https://www.facebook.com/paul.cantrell.73/

Facebook Group:https://www.facebook.com/groups/businesssuperstars/

Location: Indianapolis, Indiana, USA

In 2020 I made the shift from helping companies to helping people. Over the previous 20 years, I worked at one of the top management consulting companies in the world, PwC, helping some of the largest companies in the world improve their top line and bottom line. While there is great satisfaction in helping companies make tens and hundreds of millions of dollars, something was missing for me. I wanted to see my impact on a more personal level, improving the lives of those I work with more directly.

Also, over the last 5 years, I've dived deep into personal development learning from the greats of that industry. This helped solidify what I want out of life and how I can better use my business experience and personal growth experience to help others.

The result of all of this reflection was the creation of The Business Superstars, a coaching business dedicated to improving the lives of small business owners through personal growth, proven business tools, and the Superstars community.

I work with small business owners who want more out of their life and business. Many are feeling overwhelmed with dealing with the external influences of the pandemic, uncertainty about the future, and have lost their passion for their business. They have lost some of the drive and direction they had when they started the business and in many cases are scared that their business will even last (20% of small businesses last less than a year, 33% less than 2 years).

As a special bonus for buying Activate Your Life volume III, you can receive a free coaching call to learn more about the 7 steps you can take to grow your business or discuss a challenge you are having with your business. If you are a small business owner who wants more from your business, sign up for your free call here: www.TheBusinessSuperstars.com/activate.

Donna Cookson

Speaker, Coach, Author, Trainer, Professional Development

Website: https://www.influencemaster.net

Facebook: https://www.facebook.com/donnacookson

Instagram: https://www.instagram.com/donnacookson/

Location: Sacramento, California

Donna Cookson is a performance improvement coach, speaker, author, corporate trainer, and the President of Dale Carnegie Training in Northern California.

Donna is certified in Neuro-Linguistic Programming, Hypnosis, and Coaching, is a Master MBTI Practitioner, and has a Bachelor Degree in Law. She uses her unique combination of education, life experience, intuition, and personal rapport-building skills to create deep connections to the people she works with. She is passionate about helping her clients reach their potential and achieve their goals.

Donna works with individuals and corporate clients to develop strategic growth plans. She helps them to identify their values, passions, and possibilities. She believes deeply in her clients and provides them with tools, resources, and challenges, and aids them in creating roadmaps to success.

Dr. Karen Darke, MBE

Speaker, Author, Coach, & Paralympic Gold Medalist

Websites: www.karendarke.com ; www.quest79.com

Instagram: @handbikedarke ; @myquest79

Karen has an MBE, a Ph.D. in Geology, MA's in Development Training & High-Performance Coaching, and Diplomas in Clinical & Pastoral Counselling, Hypnotherapy & Motivational Coaching. She has been awarded honorary doctorates from The University of Aberdeen, Leeds, Cumbria, Sheffield Hallam, and Abertay Universities, in recognition of her accomplishments and contributions in adventure and sport.

Karen could be described as a modern-day alchemist. A learning and development specialist turned mindset-heartset coach, explorer, athlete, speaker, and author, Karen's purpose is about helping individuals and organizations 'find inner gold': turning challenge into opportunity.

Karen started out as a geologist researching gold in the Bolivian Andes, but a life-changing accident that left her paralyzed led her away from being a 'rock-doctor' to winning Paralympic gold in the sport of Paralympic hand-cycling in Rio 2016. It was the 79th medal for Britain, and 79 being the elemental number for Gold led to *Quest 79*, an organization supporting 'ordinary people to do extraordinary things', step out of their comfort zones and discover passion, purpose, strength, and other aspects of their 'inner gold'.

A Guinness World Record holder for land speed by arm-power, Karen loves adventures – she has skied across icecaps, kayaked at extreme latitudes of the planet, and hand-cycled across the world's biggest mountain ranges and alongside some of the longest rivers. These experiences combined with unique studies of mind, resilience, and performance have led to helping people view life as an adventure, and to embrace all its experiences as opportunities to learn and grow. Karen has extensively studied what goes on 'inside': the power of the mind and language to positively impact emotions; improving presence, performance, and wellbeing.

I have a passion for helping others transform, move beyond perceived limitations, and consider possibility. Ability is a state of mind not body: through my own journey, I have discovered the incredible power we have within us to change our thoughts, our emotions, and our energy. We can all learn to be our own alchemist, to transform unwanted emotions or experiences into gold, be creators of our reality and in doing so improve our performance, our wellbeing, and the world around us.

Yasheeka Divine

Certified Life Coach, Holistic Health & Wellness Advocate, Entrepreneur & Author

Twitter: https:www.twitter.com/urfavelifecoach

Facebook: https://www.facebook.com/urfavelifecoach

Instagram: https://www.instagram.com/lovetng1

LinkedIn:https://www.linkedin.com/in/yasheekasutton

Location: Berlin, Germany

Yasheeka was cultivated with the motto of 'excellence without excuse'. In 2009, during her tenure at Winston-Salem

State University, she founded Elle Inc. a non-profit organization empowering individuals to heal using non-conventional alternative therapies. In 2011, she became a certified life coach, followed by a two-year contract to host an international radio show *Soulful Essentials* on the Toronto-based Women's Movement Radio Network (WMRN). Followed by her contribution to the book *Love+Lifestyle Inspiration for Women* by Janet Aizenstros.

Yasheeka has been a personal coach to multi-millionaires for over 10 years using a synthesis and combination of ancient sciences & systems to guide individuals through a decision-making process. She offers private 1:1 sessions to the public as well.

Yasheeka is the founder of The Natural Guys Company, one of the newest startup companies in Berlin as highlighted during the 9th Annual Startup Night 2021. Alongside her life partner, Yasheeka formulates plant-based organic soap, salves, tinctures, and body butters from locally foraged herbs. The Natural Guys Company places value on the natural medicinal properties of plants for everyday usage, connecting people with the art of ancient healing practices.

50 Powerful Affirmations for Shifting Your Paradigm is a collection of prayers and devotion written by both Yasheeka and her life partner as a celebration for manifesting the life they want: https://www.etsy.com/listing/1034626181/50-powerful-affirmations-for-shifting

Satyavani Gayatri, Ed.D., AHP

Ayurvedic Health Practitioner, Yoga Acharya, & Spiritual Coach

Website: www.satyavanirising.com + www.zenspotinstitute.com

Telegram: @satyavanigayatri

Instagram: @satyavanigayatri

Location: Idaho

Dr. Satyavani is an Ayurvedic health practitioner, a Yoga Acharya (spiritual teacher), and a spiritual coach in the Shaivist tradition of Swami Kripalvananda.

Her signature program, *The Ayurvedic Woman*, reconnects women to their personal power through Ayurveda, Yoga, and Spirituality so they may remember who they are, what their life purpose is, and how they manifest that purpose into the world.

Dr. Satyavani is the founder of *Satyavani Rising*, her own brand dedicated to helping women step into their personal power through Ayurveda, Yoga, and Spiritual practice so they can be their most authentic selves and live their best life. She is also the co-founder of the *ZenSpot Institute for Vedic + Taoist Studies* with her husband Dr. + Taoist Priest Michael Bittner. Together they oversee the facility's training programs and wellness center that offers education and services in Traditional Indian Medicine (TIM/Ayurveda), Traditional Chinese Medicine (TCM), and modern and mystical healing and arts. Her international podcast, *The Ayurvedic Woman*, discusses all things Ayurveda, Yoga, and Spiritual practice for the purposes of living an ideal life inside and out.

Dr. Satyavani earned her doctorate in Educational Organization and Leadership with a concentration in Critical Hermeneutic theory from the University of San Francisco; an MA in Humanities from Teachers College, Columbia University; a MSEd in Educational Administration and Supervision from Pace University and a BS in History and Secondary Education from New York University. Her Ayurvedic education includes an AHP credential from New World Ayurveda, an advanced disease pathology credential from the Kerala Academy in Kerala, India, and her current work in the Ay.D (doctor of Ayurvedic medicine) program at the California College of Ayurveda. Satyavani has earned her advanced yoga teaching credential from the Kripalu Institute and her Acharya initiation in the Kripalu lineage. She is currently the founding president of the National Ayurvedic Practitioners Association.

Rachel Gladstone

Board-Certified Life & Success Coach, Clinical Hypnother-apist, EFT, NLP & T.I.M.E. Techniques Practitioner.

Facebook: https://www.facebook.com/EmbraceYourTrue-Self2020/ | https://www.facebook.com/groups/8030383071 45546/?ref=share

Instagram: https://www.instagram.com/embrace.your.true. self/

Email: Embracenlp@gmail.com

Location: Northville, Michigan USA

In my 46 years on this planet, and with God's guidance, I was able to create, manifest, and build a new, joy-filled and more soul-enriching life. I discovered the immense satisfaction of teaching others, like myself, how to love themselves completely and unconditionally. Life has so much to offer us. It is time for you too to get out there and fulfill your potential. Never stop learning and improving your life. The world is full of beautiful things to experience. I know, personally, that I will fulfill my own potential and I know that you can, too.

After surviving years of mental and physical abuse, three years ago, I finally found the strength and courage to leave my abusive/ toxic relationship. It was not easy after two attempts at killing myself, severe anxiety, and depression. I finally came to the realization that my life *did* mean something. My first step was finding an EMDR (Eye Movement Desensitization and Reprocessing) therapist, a psychotherapy technique used to treat anxiety, PTSD, and more. Instead of letting my abusive partner tear me apart and destroy me, I made different and difficult life choices that led me to seek out how I could help not only myself, but others like me. So I went back to school and now I'm a board-certified life and success coach, Clinical Hypnotherapist, EFT, NLP & T.I.M.E. Techniques Practitioner.

I follow one belief in my practice: I do not see people like the world necessarily does. I see no labels, no color, no gender, and no social status. I view humans as souls! I'm grateful to God for this journey, this life I've lived so far where I conquered so many challenges and experienced such vaste growth that ultimately led me on this path to help other lost and damaged souls. I can't imagine another more rewarding path in life.

For those of you truly seeking help, I have tools that can enhance your existing daily practices in your journey to personal growth. I can empathize with what you're going through and don't mind sharing my struggles, victories, and entire life story with you. What is your freedom, happiness, self-esteem & life worth to you?

Cassa Grant

Brand and Leadership Coach and Consultant

Instagram, Facebook, and LinkedIn: @Cassagrant

Website: www.cassagrant.com.

Cassa Grant is the creator of Wonderbrand™ and Wonder-leader,™ the coaching programs that help you SHOW UP as the kind of leader you'd want to follow.

She helps her clients communicate better, get more buy-in, and feel really great about how they're spending time in their business. They become confident leaders with unstoppable influence, unbeatable stories, and powerful personal brands.

Oh, and they get to hear about her time traveling the world and working in Antarctica, too.

Her techniques mix brand and storytelling strategy, performance coaching, and subconscious mindset work to help transform her clients from who they THINK they are into who they REALLY are so they can make their mark on the world.

Cassa is a certified NeuroLinguistic Programming Practitioner, life, and business coach.

Ian Griffith

Speaker, Coach, Author, & Mastermind Leader

Website: https://www.iancgriffith.com

Facebook: https://www.facebook.com/iancgriffith

Instagram: https://www.instagram.com/iancgriffith/

Location: Orange County, California

Ian Griffith has delivered hundreds of masterminds, work-shops, coaching sessions, seminar appearances, and training programs. Mentoring, coaching, and leading thousands of people around the world. He is a large-scale influencer with expertise in creating an audience and then adding value to their lives.

Ian is a certified coach, speaker, and founder of the company "Mindset Programs." He is also a keynote speaker, who has shared the stage with speaking legends like Joseph McClendon III.

Join Ian and his runaway success, the multi-year "Tribe of Greatness," mastermind; a program that has served hundreds with amazing speakers, great mastermind sessions, and accountability groups to make sure everyone reaches their goals and dreams.

http://www.tribeofgreatness.com

Join over 14,000 members in the powerful Facebook Group run by Ian, "Owning Greatness". This group helps you to own your greatness and gain influence over yourself and others.

http://www.owninggreatness.com

Also, you can join him for the "Online Micro Sprinting Sessions" where people not only plan their life goals, they work on their dreams together: http://www.microsprinting.com

Logan Griffith

Speaker, Coach, Author, Mastermind Leader, Course Creator, & Author

Website: http://www.logangriffith.com

Location: Orange County, California

Logan is the world's youngest mastermind leader. Logan is 10 years old and has been studying and teaching personal growth for over half his life. His mission is to help kids and adults to overcome their fear and follow their greatest dreams.

Logan has expertise in public speaking, leading masterminds, creating videos, and coaching. Logan is a junior influencer who specializes in making complicated concepts easy to understand.

Logan is the creator and leader of the Junior Mastermind. Logan's Junior Mastermind had over 25 members, and he led them for over 90 days. The 'Heroes and Monsters' concepts, created by Logan, have helped kids and adults everywhere fight the monsters that keep them from their dreams.

Logan loves teaching using live videos. Logan's videos have become viral and have reached millions of viewers. Logan also loves speaking to live audiences and has spoken dozens of times to groups that reach hundreds of members.

Logan also loves contributing to others. He loves feeding the homeless on Fridays and has done so hundreds of times. Logan made national news for his positive impact high-fiving 10,000 people in just one day. Many outstanding leaders have mentored Logan and have been on his videos; Joseph Mcclendon III, Brian Bradley, and Carolyn Rim, just to name a few.

Logan is starting his next 90 day Junior Mastermind soon. The "Junior Mastermind" is designed for kids 7-14 and you can learn more about it or join at http://www.jrmastermind.com

Join Logan in his upcoming Junior Influencer Academy. The Junior Influencer Academy integrates a Junior Influencer Mastermind, Online Course, and a 1-on-1 coaching program. This academy helps kids implement the technology, skills, and strategies needed to impact this world in a massive way. Sign up for Logan's Junior Influencer Academy or learn about Logan's upcoming Junior Influencer podcast here- http://www.juniorinfluencers.com

Logan also has an upcoming book and workshop, "Heroes and Monsters." Sign up to be a part of it at http://www.heroesfightmonsters.com

Rachel Jacobson

Eden Energy Medicine Advanced Practitioner, EFT Practitioner, Mind-Body Eating Coach, & Integrative Breathwork Facilitator

Website: www.racheljacobson.co.uk

Social Media: @holisticrachel

Location: United Kingdom

Rachel Jacobson is an advanced Eden Energy Medicine Practitioner, EFT Practitioner, Mind-Body Eating Coach, and Integrative Breathwork Facilitator. She began her journey of personal development in her late teens, first studying the nature of beliefs and consciousness, then later falling in love with the world of natural health and energy.

Rachel passionately believes that a life of wellness, vitality, and peace is available to all. From her own personal experience, she knows that life can seem like a daily struggle and that stress is a major part of life. She advocates that with simple tools and empowering knowledge, it is possible for anyone to take small steps that add up to big life changes.

Rachel offers private sessions both in-person and remotely. She also teaches regular groups and workshops.

Derek Loudermilk

Quantum Business Coach, Creator of the LEAP Method,

Host of the top-rated podcast: The Derek Loudermilk Show

Founder of AdventureQuest and the Art of Adventure,

4X Bestselling Author, *Superconductors: Revolutionize Your Career and Make Big*

Things Happen, Activate Your Life, Better Business Book

Website: Derekloudermilk.com

Location: St. Louis, Missouri/Global

Derek has coached global influencers, leading scientists, cutting-edge entrepreneurs, billionaires, world record athletes, thought leaders, NYT bestselling authors, and high achievers around the world for more than 15 years. His work has been featured in over 100 publications and podcasts globally.

Derek Loudermilk is a former pro cyclist and extreme microbiologist turned professional adventurer, author, and lifestyle entrepreneur.

His podcast, the Derek Loudermilk show, brings people to a high-level understanding of cutting-edge topics in science, spirituality, adventure, and human potential. Derek hosted the top-rated 'Art of Adventure' podcast for seven years

In 2020, Derek created the LEAP Method and the League of Superconductors - The world's first quantum business mastermind - for thought leaders shaping the New Earth.

Anahata Roach

Certified Crystal Resonance™ Therapist, Usui Reiki Master Teacher, Sekhem Seichim Reiki Master Teacher, Certified Spiral™ Practitioner, Intuitive Crystal Coach, Holistic Energy Medicine Practitioner, & Universal Life Church Minister

Website: https://thecrystalcoach.com

Social Media: @anahataroach.thecrystalcoach (FB & Instagram)

Location: St. Louis, MO, USA

As a former corporate communications executive, Anahata helps professional women who've experienced toxic relationships learn to shift away from fear and embrace self-love, thus finding balance, peace, and energy.

A certified Crystal Resonance™ Therapist since 2011, Anahata's knowledge of crystals and stones has helped her cli-

217

ents and students to release outdated programming on a cellular level and restore energetic balance to the body. Anahata can guide you through a process to permanently delete old emotional patterns and programs, while offering crystal coaching for integrating the dramatic shift in energies. She also provides clients with guidance, information, and clarity through intuitive readings.

Although a city dweller, Anahata's rural childhood gave her an appreciation for the little things that nature offers to those who seek them. She currently lives across the street from one of the largest US public parks and feeds her soul with regular walks there.

Teacher, intuitive and holistic energy medicine practitioner, Anahata Roach is The Crystal Coach!

Sonia K. Singh

Internationally Certified Leadership and High-Performance Coach offering courses, mastermind programs, and workshops

Website: InfluentialLeadershipAcademy.com

Social Media: @SoniaSinghInternational

Location: Bay Area, CA, USA

Sonia is the CEO of Sonia Singh International, a training, coaching, and consulting firm, founder of the Influential Leadership Academy, and a university professor. She teaches business leaders how to solve problems, build emotional intelligence, and accelerate their success.

Sonia believes that leadership isn't about who has the loudest voice or even how much you know. Regardless of your title, your background, or whether you're an introvert or extrovert, everyone has the potential to be an inspiring and influential leader.

Her signature program, Master Your Influence: Solve Problems Faster, Get Noticed,

Make an Impact, helps professionals gain the confidence, focus, and tools they need to transform their careers.

Sonia holds a degree in Psychology from Northern Illinois University, a master's degree in Management from Tulane University, and is certified by the International Coaching Federation.

Glenn Valentin

Master in Physiotherapy and Movement Sciences, & Social Freedom Coach

Website: www.smileplaygive.com

Facebook: facebook.com/glenn.valentin.336

Location: Planet Earth

Glenn Valentin is a curious inhabitant of planet earth who adventures in the domains of endurance sports, writing, health promotion, and social freedom. Glenn is also a recovering physiotherapist, the job he left because he felt unsatisfied in a medical system that's focused on treating symptoms instead of causes, and - more importantly - because his awkwardness needed a creative outlet.

In 2020, Glenn climbed the *Col du Tourmalet*, one of the most mythical mountain passes of the Tour de France, on a spacehopper. Later that year, he became the world's first person to cross a mountain range (the Pyrenees) with a unicorn. From that moment on, Glenn was hooked on embracing his weirdness and started doing social experiments such as dancing in the streets of Brussels, handing out roses to girls he wanted to date on Valentine's Day, and asking strangers what their dreams in life are. In 2021, Glenn broke the Guinness World Record for the greatest distance traveled on a spacehopper in one day.

Currently, Glenn is looking for social freedom buddies who want to help him make the world a more smiling, playing, and giving place. Visit his website www.smileplaygive.com to get in touch.

Justin Wenck

Qualifications/ Services: Teacher, Speaker, Coach, Podcaster, and Problem Solver

Website: https://www.justinwenck.com/

Facebook: https://www.facebook.com/justinwenckphd

Instagram: https://www.instagram.com/justinwenckphd/

LinkedIn: http://www.linkedin.com/in/justinwenck

Location: Sacramento, California

Short Bio:

Justin Wenck, Ph.D. is an expert in working with the most complex system and programming in the world: your mind.

He began with computers over 25 years ago, earning a doctorate in Electrical Engineering. 15 years ago he became dedicated to unlocking the magic of the mind using modern scientific methods and traditional yoga and meditation techniques. His mission is to make it easy for anyone to transform their life using the simple, yet powerful tools of his PLS method so they can experience a life of less stress, more energy, and passion.

Justin's quest for fulfilment beyond success began in 2015 when he had just gotten promoted after working as a circuit designer for CPUs for five years, and he was effectively succeeding in his dream job that he set out to do from age 15. There was just one problem: he was miserable. He didn't see how he'd grow. He was fed up working with the same five people on his team. In short: he didn't want to be there anymore.

He made it his mission to go beyond success to fulfillment. He read books. He talked to coworkers and friends. He hired coaches and took trainings. This was the beginning of his journey to creating the PLS method and tools for transformation. He's been using tools of this method to achieve the following professional roles:

- SSD Validation Lead 2015

- Technical Marketing Engineer 2017

- Marketing Engineering Manager 2018

- Product Engineering Lead 2019

- Host and Creator The Engineering Emotions and Energy Podcast 2019

- Founder E-motions Engineering 2020

Additional credentials:

- Certified Practitioner of SuperHuman Interaction Technology, Human Communications Institute, 2019.

- Certified Practitioner of Human Interaction Technology, Human Communications Institute, 2015.

- Leader at Human Communications Institute seminars on communication, confidence, commitment, congruence, and rapport skills.

- Emcee and Speaker for events with up to 500+ attendees.

- Certified Yoga Teacher.

He's taught the PLS method to co-workers, friends, and clients to set them up for lives of less stress, more energy, and passion, and now he's excited to bring it to you.

Ditte Young

Spiritual Coaching, Animal Communication, Therapy, Clairvoyance, & Mediumship

Website: www.ditteyoung.com | www.d-evelopment.com

Social Media: www.facebook.com/Developmentgruppe/

Instagram: @ditteyoung & @ditteyoung.international

Location: Denmark

Ditte Young was born with the special gifts of a luxurious amount of energy and detailed information given to her from the spiritual world. It has required strength, courage, discipline, and focus to go out in public since the year 1999, sharing spiritual information to human beings and animal owners.

She is a spiritual coach using all the best from her studies as a psychotherapist, her experience as a coach, healer, animal communicator, and clairvoyant. She specialized in shock and trauma, the nervous system, stress, and conflicts in relationships and has a great interest in working with families especially within the spectrum of autism.

Ditte also helps business owners with increased revenues, strategies, and setting goals that resonate with their hearts and souls. She also helps private persons with readings online or by mail all over the world.

She is the most famous animal communicator in Scandinavia and has taught her telepathic skills to more than 400 students in various countries. She works with elite riders helping them setting and reaching their goals in all branches of the equine industry, from the pony-loving girl to the Olympic rider.

Ditte is the author of 3 books, published by her publisher as paperbacks, audio books, and e-books. She also has her own podcast series and goes out to shows, clinics, and other performances sharing her knowledge to people who find relationships and inner personal growth interesting. She is the leader of many spiritual coaching mentorship workshops for women all over the country too.

Tami Zenoble

Group and Individual Biofield Tuning Sessions, Shamanic Journey Workshops, Sound and Shamanism Workshops and Retreats, Fire Ceremony, Land Ceremony.

Website: https://phoenixmoonretreats.com/

Facebook: https://www.facebook.com/Phoenixmoonus

Instagram: https://www.instagram.com/phoenixmoon_us/

Location: Oregon

After closing my business in 2015 to have rotator cuff surgery, I sought transformation. My name is Tami Zenoble and I have owned my own practice as a Certified Massage Therapist, a Level 1 Reiki Practitioner, and Licensed Esthetician for 15 years. After recovering from the surgery, I moved to Oregon with the intention of transforming my life into something that powerfully matched my heart's desire. In May of 2018, I was drawn to a Shamanic Journeying workshop led by Hank Wesselman. After that workshop, I realized I wanted ed to share that sacred transformational space with others, to facilitate access to information that would transform and empower them to live more authentically and in alignment with their life purpose.

Since then, I have been using this practice to co-create my life with the Universe. The study of Shamanism has given me a new perspective and has allowed me to discover the very thing I was seeking. I am amazed at what life shows me each and every day. Today, I am continuing my life-long studies with Sandra Ingerman and Alerto Villoldo, as Hank is no longer with us.

Recently, I discovered the energy balancing technique of Biofield Tuning. At the end of 2020, I was receiving sessions via the internet, to cope with the stress and uncertainty of the pandemic. It was during one of these sessions I realized how similar it was to the energy balancing techniques I practiced as a massage therapist. It was then that I knew I wanted to combine Shamanic Journey work with Biofield Tuning to empower people in bringing about the transformation they are seeking on a deep spiritual and energetic level. I now offer workshops and retreats doing this very thing.

To assist you on your journey, download a very special, 10 minute Shamanic drumming and rattling track, recorded live at Breitenbush Hot Springs, when you subscribe to my email list: @PhoenixMoonRetreats.com.

Rong Zhao

Speaker and Peak Performance Coach offering classes, group coaching programs, and workshops

Social media:

- FB: https://www.facebook.com/ron.zhao.5/

- Instagram: https://www.instagram.com/the.rongway/

- Website: https://www.therongway.com/

Location: California/Colorado

Rong is a speaker, peak performance coach, and stand-up comedian. He's a certified NLP master practitioner and hypnotherapist, specializing in emotion control, confidence & motivation, and belief change work. He's frequently on stage in front of a crowds from 10 to 200+ people. Through coaching and speaking, Rong has helped transform hundreds of people's lives.

Rong believes that everything we want to change in life comes down to changing our thoughts and feelings. When we realize we have the power to change our beliefs and emotions, we find peace and joy within.

His signature workshop - "The Journey to Empowerment" teaches individuals how to take control of their emotions and discover their self-empowerment.

Rong is fortunate enough to be coached and trained by some of the greatest leaders in personal development, including Tony Robbins, John Maxwell, Master Co, Wim Hoff, Jack Canfield, Igor Ledochowski, Connirae Andreas, Tim Hall-bom/Kris Hallbom, Robert Dilts, etc.

Dr. Jimmy McDowell (aka Dr. Golden Boy)

Dentist, Professional Wrestler, Actor, Author, Entrepreneur, Motivational Speaker!

Instagram: @drgoldenboydds

Facebook: Jim McDowell / DrJimmyMcDowell

Website: DrJDMcDowell@aol.com

"I help empower people to become their ultimate persona!"

After a successful and acclaimed high school and college football career, I felt a lifelong calling to become a dentist. In becoming a cosmetic dentist of a top 1% dental practice in the US, I attracted Hollywood actors, NFL, NBA, PGA, and MLB Hall of Famers as patients. I helped transform their smiles!

During their transformations, I felt a new persona coming out from deep inside my core. I now wanted to become a Professional Wrestler! I found my new persona in the mirror on my wall. I saw it, focused on it, and I became it. I am now a renowned Heavyweight Champion in many wrestling organizations.

With that example, I started helping others attain a level of empowered persona to blitz their markets with electric success. Inside a short time, many saw themselves as the perfect answer to what they visualized looking into their mirror. So, become your ultimate Persona w/ Dr. Jimmy McDowell as your coach, motivator, teacher, who turns your life into a journey using "Mirror, Mirror on the Wall!" as your new you!

In my personal life, I am the dad of 4 amazing daughters and 1 son. Being their loving role model was a goal of mine from day one. They can now look into their mirror and see the reflection of their dad. I worked hard to share that love with a nurturing heart. Now, as they lead their families, the circle of life has begun again.

Diane Hopkins

Book Writing Coach, Nonfiction Book Editor, TED/TEDx Speech Editor

Instagram: @wordandwing

Facebook: /wordandwing

Website: wordandwing.co

Diane Hopkins, Ph.D is a book writing coach and nonfiction editor. She is the editor of this book, and the previous two editions of Activate Your Life, Vol 1 and Vol 2.

A trained university professor, speaker, and author, she now helps coaches and entrepreneurs find their voice on the page and get their books written. She specializes in guiding people to write self-help, nonfiction, and memoir books. Diane has also helped her clients craft powerful speeches for United Nations presentations, TED Women and TEDx talks, and international conferences.

Diane is a lover of the written and spoken word and is the go-to person when it comes to getting your message out to bigger audiences. Working with people one-on-one or teaching workshops and retreats, she shows aspiring authors how to tell their stories and share their expertise in a way that inspires powerful change in the lives of their audience.

Diane helps you tap into your deepest, most authentic truth and overcome your fears about sharing it so you can step forward into your rightful place as the confident thought leader you're destined to be.